Creating a
VICTORIAN
Flower Garden

Creating a VICTORIAN Flower Garden

STEFAN BUCZACKI

Original flower paintings by
Alice Drummond-Hay

Weidenfeld & Nicolson
New York

Published by Weidenfeld & Nicolson, New York
A Division of Wheatland Corporation
841 Broadway
New York, New York 10003-4793

First published in Great Britain in 1988 by
William Collins Sons & Co. Ltd.

The publishers are grateful to the following sources for the use of their illustrations:
The Bridgeman Art Library/Christopher Wood Gallery: pages 37, 57, 69.
The Bridgeman Art Library/City of New York Art Gallery: page 13.
Harry Smith Horticultural Photographic Library: pages 59, 71.
Mary Evans Picture Library: page 12.   National Portrait Gallery: page 56.
Thompson, J., *The Gardener's Assistant*, 1888: page 49.

Other sources: Cassells *Popular Gardening*, Vol III.
Drury, W.D., *The Book of Gardening*, 1900.   *Garden Work*, 1887.
Glenny, G., *The Flower Garden and Greenhouse*, 1851
Hibberd, S., *The Amateur's Greenhouse and Conservatory*, 1873;
The Amateur's Flower Garden, 1871; *Profitable Gardening*, 1860.
Hughes, J., *Garden Architecture and Landscape Gardening*, 1866.
The Illustrated London News, 1851.
Robinson, W., *The English Flower Garden*, 1883; *The English
Flower Garden*, 1911; *The Wild Garden*, 1903.
Royal Horticultural Society Journal, 1943.
Smee, A., *My Garden*, 1872.   Suttons Seed Catalogues, 1890-1900.

The charmingly illustrated birthday and other greetings cards shown on
page 2 were painted by Alice Drummond-Hay and sent to members of her family.

Library of Congress Cataloging-in-Publication Data

Buczacki, S.T.
      Creating a Victorian flower garden/by Stefan Buczacki. – 1st ed.
         p.   cm.
      Bibliography: p.
      Includes index.
      ISBN 1-555-84285-2
      1. Gardens, Victorian. 2. Gardening. 3. Plants, Ornamental.
      4. Drummond-Hay, Alice, 1865-1956. 5. Gardens, Victorian –
      Great Britain. 6. Gardening – Great Britain – History. 7. Plants,
      Ornamental – Great Britain.   I. Title.
      SB458.7.B83   1988
      712'.6'0941 – dc19   88-10340
                                                                                    CIP

Designed by Steven Wooster

Set in Bodoni Book 504 by Chambers Wallace, London
Color origination by Alpha Reprographics Ltd.
Printed and bound by William Collins Sons & Co. Ltd., Glasgow.

First American Edition
10 9 8 7 6 5 4 3 2 1

CONTENTS

FOREWORD

Early in 1985, I found my long-held interest in garden history being brought very much to the front of my thoughts. I had recently moved from a house and garden of 1870 to one that probably started life early in the 1600s. I was faced with the same problem in both gardens, for while there was no intention in either case of entirely re-creating a garden of the period, I did want a range of appropriate plants. Yet information on their availability was scant and scattered. Then, in one of life's coincidences, my publishers showed me an album of flower paintings made around 1890 and that had been sent to them from a family in Scotland. I was asked what I thought of the paintings and if they merited publication.

The flower album had been painted by a Perthshire lady named Alice Drummond-Hay. Her family had appreciated its quality and kept it safely, only taking it out occasionally to show to interested visitors. The paintings were a joy to see and as I turned the album pages I was struck first by their great beauty and freshness; and second by their evident botanical accuracy and scope. Yes, of course they merited publication, but we could see no justification for yet another book of attractive old flower paintings, good as they were, unless they could be put to serve some useful purpose. So what better way to use them than to illustrate a book that guided a gardener into the re-creation of a garden of the 1890s?

It has seemed that we touched a live topic for an interest in Victorian gardening seems suddenly to have become fashionable. But while the fascinating techniques used a century ago in the kitchen garden are of limited practical use, a flower garden is a very different matter. This can actually be re-created anywhere. And it is to enable a modern gardener, with whatever space available, to re-create a Victorian style of flower garden using appropriate plants, that I have written the book.

This is not a manual for museum gardening – I see no point in using outmoded techniques but I do believe that anyone sufficiently interested in

Victorian gardens to want to grow some plants of the period will also be interested to know something of the ways in which they would have been handled then. Although I have, of course, concentrated on the nineteenth century, and on the latter part especially, I give a brief summary of British gardening history leading up to Queen Victoria's coronation in 1837. Although the book is based on the plants to be found in a British garden of the period, many of its features were those of North American gardens too and there is no reason why the plants could not be grown in a re-created Victorian style of garden anywhere with a roughly comparable climate. Indeed, many of the plants popular in British gardens then had been fairly recently introduced from North America.

The last chapter in the book is the largest and is given over to a directory of the most important flowers and flowering shrubs of the late Victorian garden. I have indicated appropriate varieties and suggested where modern ones could or could not substitute. The descriptions in the directory are cross-referenced to the plates of Alice Drummond-Hays's paintings and I have also included a number of plants important at the time but which she did not illustrate, presumably because they did not grow in her own garden. Almost all of the illustrations apart from the plates are taken from nineteenth-century books or magazines. Although Alice painted her album more or less as a seasonal record, we have rearranged some of the plates to make them more readily applicable to the directory entries.

The handwriting on some of the plates is either in Alice Drummond-Hay's hand or one of the family's. The names are, of course, those current in 1890 but the identifications are all sound. Almost all of the unnamed plants can be identified reasonably accurately because of the preciseness of Alice's paintings. Nonetheless, there remain a few over which I have drawn a blank and I have indicated them as 'Unidentified'. If anyone can suggest names, I shall be delighted to hear from them.

Helleborus Abchasicus
Abchasian Hellebore
I

III
Hamamelisaberia
Japanese Witch-
-Hazel-

II
Tussilago fragrans
Winter Heliotrope

Galanthus
Snowdrop
IV

V

Eranthus
-Hyemalis-
Winter-Aconite

I *Helleborus abchasicus* · Abchasian hellebore
II *Tussilago fragrans* · Winter heliotrope
III *Hamamelis aberia* · Japanese witch hazel
IV *Galanthus (nivalis)* · Snowdrop **V** *Eranthis hyemalis* · Winter aconite

CHAPTER I

ALICE
DRUMMOND-HAY

Lieutenant Colonel Henry Maurice Drummond-Hay.

The Drummond-Hay children with their mother, Charlotte, on the front steps at Seggieden in about 1900. Back row (left to right): Lucy, Henry, James; middle row (left to right): Alice, Edith, Charlotte; front row: Constance.

TRAVELLING EAST from Perth along the main road to Dundee, you trace the course of the lower reaches of the River Tay and the north shore of the Firth of Tay, through country that is the ancestral home of the Hays. To the south of the river is Moncrieff land while behind you is Murray territory and, beyond that, a large rambling tract of Drummond country. The road passes through the fertile river flood plain of the Carse of Gowrie, a region steeped in the rich and often bloody history of Scotland, but today the visitor will find it an unexpectedly gentle and intimate landscape of rolling hills and mixed farming. Close by Glencarse village, on the banks of the Tay, lies the sheltered locality of Seggieden or Suggeden, a name derived from the Gaelic and variously translated as 'overgrown with reeds' or the 'willow den'.

A short way downstream from Seggieden is the site of a small pier, once known as 'The Ferry of the Loaf'. This was mentioned by Sir Walter Scott in 'The Fair Maid of Perth' and is said to be the spot where Macduff, the Thane of Fife, crossed the Tay pursued by Macbeth's men. Being short of money, Macduff had nothing to give the Seggieden ferryman except a loaf of bread that he had taken from the King's table when fleeing Dunsinane castle. This crossing of the Tay is also believed to be part of the old Coronation route followed by the ancient kings of Scotland on their way to be enthroned at the nearby village of Scone, whose famous stone was removed to Westminster Abbey by Edward I in 1296.

SEGGIEDEN AND THE DRUMMOND-HAYS

As long ago as the thirteenth century a hospital existed at Seggieden under the care of Augustinian monks. Its ultimate fate is not known although it was certainly thriving in 1559. Subsequently, however, a branch of the Hay family had a house on the site, only to see it burned during the Jacobite Rebellion of 1745. Sometime within the succeeding fifty years, a replacement house was built in the Adam style and it is this mansion that figures centrally in our present interest.

8

The Hay mansion was restrained, modest as country residences go but beautifully proportioned and comfortable. There were good salmon in the river and the Hay family flourished. In 1859, Charlotte, the daughter and heiress of the recently deceased laird of Seggieden, Captain James Richardson-Hay, married one of the Drummonds: Henry Maurice Drummond. He was a 45-year-old Captain of the 42nd Royal Highlanders (the Black Watch) and later Lieutenant Colonel of the Royal Perthshire Rifle Militia, and the youngest son of Admiral Sir Adam Drummond of Megginch and his wife, Lady Charlotte, daughter of the fourth Duke of Atholl (the man who, with his forebears, was responsible for the widespread introduction of the larch tree to British forestry). On his marriage, Henry Drummond changed his name to Drummond-Hay and took up residence at Seggieden.

The Drummond-Hays were thus a well-bred and moderately wealthy family and through the influence of Colonel Henry, natural history was a family passion. He studied birds, fish and plants both on his travels abroad and at home, became Honorary Curator and then President of the Museum of the Perthshire Society of Natural Science and left a herbarium and a prodigious collection of stuffed birds, the latter still on display at Megginch Castle despite some losses in a disastrous fire in 1969.

The Drummond-Hays had six children: two sons, James and Henry, and four daughters, Constance, Alice, Lucie and Edith. None of the girls married, and to judge by surviving family albums and scrapbooks, probably because none of them had time. They were industrious women, much given to good works and, in the custom of the time, became accomplished in such pursuits as embroidery and painting. Art was clearly a considerable interest and family talent – Constance painted a fine series of illustrations of fungi now at the Royal Botanic Gardens, Edinburgh, while Edith produced an astonishing collection of illustrated diaries charting the family's history over many years. These include such delightful vignettes as those depicting a local visit by Queen Victoria, to whom Alice was presented at Holyrood House, the royal palace in Edinburgh.

Alice Drummond-Hay as a young woman.

ALICE DRUMMOND-HAY

Alice, the third child and second daughter, born in 1865, was perhaps the most industrious and also the most talented painter of all. In addition to her flower albums, she produced flowery family greetings cards, was a pianist with a special fondness for Scottish music, produced amateur dramatics, studied languages, took lengthy visits with her sisters to friends and relatives and made journeys to France and Switzerland – all carefully chronicled by Edith.

Alice was a devout churchwoman, giving much time and energy to the local Episcopalian church at Glencarse, built in 1878 with her father contributing substantially towards the cost. The sisters were clearly the mainstays of the community, taking Sunday School classes, playing the organ and running the choir for over sixty years. During the First World War, Alice was a nurse in the Voluntary Aid Detachment with the Red Cross in Perth. When their mother died in 1914, the sisters left the family home at Seggieden and later had a house, 'St Kessogs', built for them in Glencarse village, close by the church. The house remains in the family still and Alice lived there, much loved locally and always known to the family as 'Aunt Ally' until her death at the

Seggie Den, Glencarse

The south front of Seggieden in its prime, with climbers, conservatory and well-tended flower beds.

Seggieden from the south, facing the river Tay.

age of ninety in 1956. She is remembered as a kindly gentle person with a lively sense of humour and with 'a preference for the colour purple and for the wearing of long tartan skirts'.

THE GARDEN AT SEGGIEDEN

But I must return to Seggieden and to the 1880s and 1890s when the garden was at its height and when Alice drew inspiration from it to record the flowers and create the paintings reproduced here. The paintings were contained in a single album, produced as far as can be judged from family information around 1890 or 1891, a view supported by the absence from it of any plants introduced to British gardens after that date. Judging by the plants illustrated and by photographs taken slightly later, the garden contained most of the features that might be expected of a small country house garden of the period although there is little evidence of much planting of formal bedding. This was probably because Colonel Henry's fondness for natural history led him to become a disciple of the approach to gardening led by William Robinson and Gertrude Jekyll; certainly there were hardly any bedding plants in Alice's

record – such important Victorian flowers as pelargoniums, alonsoas and heliotropiums, for instance, are absent. Interestingly, aerial photographs taken later in the 1930s do reveal rather extensive bedding schemes, including apparently some regimental crest designs on the south side of the house overlooking the Tay. Despite the earlier absence of bedding plants, there were certainly some exciting and unexpected plants there at the end of the nineteenth century – *Jasminum humile* and *Trillium grandiflorum*, for instance.

The absence of a few popular shrubs or herbaceous plants that might have been expected can be explained either by the local soil, which is markedly acid, or by the climate, which can be harsh in winter. The album of paintings was clearly intended as a month by month and season by season record, although the latter part of the year is less complete and Alice's hand-written plant names are not as thoroughly entered towards the end. Her botanical observations are for the most part very accurate and only occasionally has a flower been recorded slightly incorrectly. The identifications are sound too, but this may reflect more her father's knowledge and labelling. There

10

is no record of the garden staff at Seggieden, but almost certainly Alice and her sisters played a part in the gardening activities.

And what of Seggieden today? After the Second World War, the house was considerably modernized by James Drummond-Hay and his family – electricity and bathrooms were installed. Between 1945 and 1958, Lady Margaret Drummond-Hay ran it as a school but later, in the 1960s, dry rot was discovered to be so extensive as to make the building unsafe – the dining room ceiling was held aloft for a long time by scaffolding. The cost of restoration would clearly have been prodigious and the end was inevitable. The last resident, James Drummond-Hay, built a small modern house in the grounds which his family still own. The National Monuments Record of Scotland photographed the old property in 1970 and a regulated fire was intended to bring about its demise in three stages. Unfortunately, the fire was soon out of hand, it spread from the wing under the dome and the old house burned uncontrolled for three or four days before the bulldozers finished the job. The mansion of Seggieden, built with care in the 1700s and a much-loved family home for generations, was gone.

THE INSPIRATION LIVES ON

When I visited the site in the summer of 1986, I could still recognize many of the old rhododendrons that lined the drive and find several of the fine conifers that were the remains of the old Colonel's arboretum. Through an ancient door, I entered the walled garden, most of it overgrown, the old propagating house just discernible beneath a tangle of wild Perthshire vegetation. The ground was littered with broken glass and here and there ancient fruit trees were the only testimonies to the thriving family community of years past. The house itself had been completely razed and only in my mind's eye could I re-create its image – the hall with 'the great fire burning in a huge stove in this circular grey-carpeted room, the cream walls reaching to a gallery above, lit by a beautifully shaped oval cupola'. Or the dining room – 'panelled with wood to the ceiling, with crimson brocade curtains and pelmets, a thick green carpet and a fine old Chippendale sideboard, and chairs covered in dark crimson'. Where once 'arranged on the grey marble mantlepiece' were 'some beautiful pieces of sculpture and on the walls old portraits and Italian and Flemish paintings', knotted brambles and couch grass reigned supreme. Exploring on top of the rubble site where the elevated position suggested the views that Alice enjoyed from her room overlooking the Tay, I stumbled over a cylindrical stone fragment that in its parallel fluting revealed itself as part of one of the Greek columns that once graced the entrance porch. *Sic transit.*

But in Alice's flowers, hidden from the light and retaining their freshness for almost a century, the garden of Seggieden lives on. In recording their colours for posterity, she has given us the inspiration to envisage their perfumes, to imagine the bright dappled light of long-gone summers and the crisp frosty mornings of the Perthshire winters of her youth. As you turn the pages and think of kind, gentle Aunt Ally, be inspired to re-create a little of the glory of the Victorian gardens she knew and in so doing, make a living memorial to a very talented lady.

In a state of poor repair, the house was photographed for the National Monuments Record of Scotland in 1970.

CHAPTER II

THE VICTORIAN GARDEN

IT ENDED but two and a half generations ago. There are still people alive who remember spending their childhood in it. Yet the Victorian age began only twenty one years after the Battle of Waterloo and only thirty two years after Nelson's victory at Trafalgar. Victoria's reign was certainly the longest in British history but, within its sixty three years, Britain and the world of which Britain was in many ways the hub changed beyond imagining. For this was the age of the Industrial Revolution, the coming of massive machinery, of coal, steam and the power they bestowed. It was, in consequence, the age in which communication and transport underwent their own revolution, when the world suddenly shrank and far-flung places were hauled a little closer to home. It has been called 'a golden age' and undeniably it saw Britain at the height of her powers. There were, nonetheless, still marked divisions within society; the poor man in his cottage was still poor, while both the old rich in their country estates and the new rich in their mansions grew richer.

When the 18-year-old Princess Alexandrina Victoria acceded to the throne on 20 June 1836, little could she have realized what lay ahead or that her name would bestow a new adjective on her native tongue. The word 'Victorian' to modern ears means many things – old-fashioned, conservative or prudish to some, stately or regal to

The young Queen Victoria in 1841, four years after she came to the throne.

others – but there is scarcely a walk of life, a field of human activity or endeavour that does not have a branch or facet dubbed Victorian. And so it is with horticulture and with gardening. While the casual observer might be excused for thinking of Victorian horticulture solely in terms of the traditional English cottage garden, there is much, very much more to it than that. For what rendered the period of especial interest relative to other periods in gardening history was that it coincided with the expansion of the British Empire.

The British Empire at its height was the largest administrative entity the world has ever seen; by Victoria's death in 1901, it spanned about a

An English Garden *by P. Craft.*

quarter of the land surface of the earth. It comprised deserts and prairies, monsoon lands and mountain ranges, tropical rain forests and tundras. It included, moreover, the natural habitats of a fairly large proportion of the flowering plants of the world. But perhaps more significantly still, the countries of the Empire were stepping stones to even more richly floriferous lands. From India it was a short but breath-stopping scramble to Nepal and the Himalayas, while from Hong Kong, Malaya and Burma routes stretched into the botanical storehouse of China.

The expansion of the Empire spurred adventurers and explorers to comb the planet for its bounties; and those Britons whose principal enthusiasm was for botany and horticulture shipped back to their homeland such a richness of plant life as had never before been seen in one place at one time. And as the British Isles has as good an overall climate for gardening and plant raising as can be found, in such a restricted region, anywhere else in the world, it was small wonder that the Victorian gardening environment was singularly endowed.

OVERSEAS INTRODUCTIONS

Among the numberless plants introduced to Britain during the Victorian period were *Weigela*, the yellow flowered winter jasmine, *Mahonia japonica*, *Forsythia*, Japanese anemone and Japanese quince. All (and many others) were collected by Robert Fortune in the space of a few mid-century years in the Far East. Tuberous begonias were brought back from South America for Veitch's nursery by Richard Pearce; *Primula obconica* was found in the Far East by Charles Maries, and a most glorious group of shrubs and climbers was collected in Chile by William Lobb – *Tropaeolum speciosum*, *Desfontainea spinosa*, *Embothrium coccineum*, *Lapageria rosea*, and, perhaps most glorious of all, *Berberis darwinii*; and there were many, many more. It is said, for instance, that the number of orchid species at the Royal Botanic Gardens at Kew was multiplied one thousand times in the first fifty years of the nineteenth century as collector after collector sent home their findings.

Although many humbler bedding and border plants, too, were nineteenth-century introductions, it was through the ever developing techniques of plant hybridization (or 'improvement' as it was known popularly) that they made their greatest impact. It is a fact too often taken for granted that the modern seedsman's catalogue is very largely a catalogue of hybrids; and complex hybrids at that. Take petunias, for example; wild species were probably introduced into cultivation in the sixteenth century but they were not hybridized until the 1830s. The early simple hybrids or colour selections were often named as if they were true species; James Carter's catalogue for 1849, for instance, listed *Petunia phoenicea*, *P. violacea*, *P. alba*, *P. blockii*, *P. grandiflora*, *P. picta*, *P. rosea*, *P. striata* and *P. nyctaginiflora*, whereas in the catalogue of the seed company that owns the James Carter brand today will be found F_1 hybrid Single Multifloras, such as the Resisto series or the Formula Mixtures, F_1 hybrid Doubles and F_1 hybrid Grandifloras, again in a range of named varieties. But if you add to the natural features of British soil and British gardening weather a few other significant nineteenth-century developments, you have, indeed, a horticultural hotbed. Perhaps most importantly, there had been a tax on glass in Britain since the end of the seventeenth century and by the time Queen Victoria was a girl, its cost had become almost prohibitive. After several reductions, the wretched levy was eventually repealed in 1845 and greenhouse building was given a phenomenal impetus. Ever-improving methods of steam generation to provide greenhouse heat further stimulated at least

Weigela coraeensis, *introduced to Britain from Japan around 1850.*

Chaenomeles japonica, *introduced to Britain from Japan in 1869.*

Jasminum nudiflorum, *introduced to Britain from China by the great plant collector Robert Fortune in 1844.*

I *Ilex aquifolium* · Golden berried holly
II *Jasminum nudiflorum* · Winter jasmine
III *Primula vulgaris* · Primroses   IV *Ilex aquifolium* · Common holly
V *Chaenomeles japonica (= Pyrus japonica)* · Japan apple tree, Japanese quince

I Garrya elliptica **II** Viola sp. · Czar violet **III** Viola sp. · Neapolitan violet
IV Hepatica nobilis (= Triloba rubra = Anemone hepatica) **V** Cotoneaster simonsii **VI** Arabis albida · White arabis
VII Crocus imperati **VIII** Narcissus sp. · Daffodil **IX** Anemone blanda **X** Helleborus purpurascens
XI Crocus sieberi

I *Cheiranthus cheiri* · Wallflower   II *Pieris (= Andromeda) floribunda*   III *Crocus* (garden hybrids) · Large Dutch crocus
IV *Heleborus olympicus*   V *Bellis perennis* · Double daisy   VI *Muscari botryoides* · Grape hyacinth   VII *Viola* sp. · Pansy
VIII *Erica herbacea* · Winter heather   IX *Primula × polyantha* · Polyanthus

the more wealthy to indulge their horticultural fantasies to the full. And, finally, there was built up a fund of gardening expertise the like of which has not been seen before or since. Every gentleman worthy of the name had his own garden staff, working under and trained by a head gardener who had in turn received his schooling at one of the great houses of the time. From the astonishing royal gardens at Frogmore near Windsor, where over one hundred garden staff laboured to serve the horticultural (and gastronomic) demands of the Queen's household, to the (relatively) humble country rectory with one gardener and a boy, the nation's gardens were of a standard never to be matched. Truly, for a gardener, plantsman or botanist, the nineteenth century was a time to be alive.

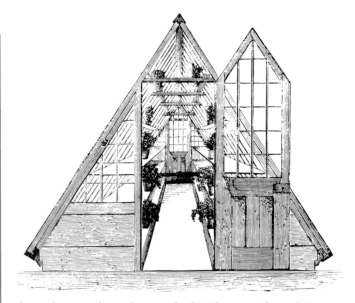

A mid-nineteenth century glasshouse based on a design by Paxton.

THE EARLIEST GARDENS

To understand the Victorian garden and the gardening environment in Victorian Britain, we must step backwards and put those sixty or so years in the context of what had gone before. It is impossible to point a finger at a precise date in history when British gardening began. There are several reasons for this. First, although today we tend to understand by 'gardening' the cultivation of plants close to a home for the occupants' personal use rather than for trade or sale, the distinction between gardening and farming was for long blurred. Second, the bulk of gardening today tends to be the cultivation of ornamental rather than food crops, and this shift in relative importance is a fairly recent phenomenon. And third, of course, documentary evidence from the earliest periods of plant cultivation in the British Isles is scant. Nonetheless, it is known that by the eleventh and twelfth centuries, the sanctuaries of learning and of worship and the homes of the nobility boasted gardens where vegetables, vines and other fruits, herbs both culinary and medicinal, and unashamedly ornamental plants such as roses and other familiar flowers, were raised. To modern eyes and in modern terms, these were formal gardens, predominantly planned by the

draughtsman's ruler and dividers and making ample and significant use of non-living features such as stonework and gravel. But the degree of sophistication employed was remarkable; for instance, there were dealers in lawn turf in the late thirteenth century, over 500 years before the invention of the lawn mower.

The grand-scale pleasure garden, in contrast to the purely functional garden, first seems to have assumed importance from the late fifteenth century onwards. Henry VIII was the most celebrated supporter of gardening activity at the time and his palaces at Hampton Court, Nonsuch and Whitehall were embellished with gardens of which the principal features were Tudor knots – series of elaborately designed geometric beds bordered with rosemary, lavender, cotton lavender, box or other low-growing and easily managed shrubs, and incorporating coloured earth and gravel in addition to plants. Seen from above, the whole offered a remarkable similarity to a pattern of knotted ropes. To enable them to be seen from above, the beds in gardens of the period were laid out beneath the windows of the great house or close to a raised bank, or mount, from which the whole could be surveyed and admired.

Changes, however, were afoot, for new ideas arrived in the land as a result of a more peaceful Europe and the increase in foreign travel. By the early seventeenth century, the British garden literally opened out from its enclosures, mainly as a result of Italian influences. Huge radiating avenues, vistas, grottos, classical statuary, elaborate parterres and water – water almost everywhere, cascading and fountaining – became *de rigueur*. After the interruption of the English Civil War, the evolution continued and in the latter part of the seventeenth century, the dominant influences were French and to some degree Dutch, rather than Italian.

THE LANDSCAPE REVOLUTION

Eventually, in the early eighteenth century, something indigenous was created. William Kent, Humphry Repton, Lancelot 'Capability' Brown, Henry Hoare and other British gardeners devised an art form that was both dynamic yet abiding – the landscaped park. Environments in many ways more akin to tropical savannahs than to temperate climate landscapes lapped up to sunken 'ha-ha' ditches, bringing a reconstituted countryside within a stone's throw of the drawing room. Hills were moved, rivers dammed, and trees, native and exotic, planted by the tens of thousands. Nevertheless, even in 1730, those among the King's subjects who could afford such grandeur were few indeed and the landscape movement in fact had little effect on the smaller country house gardens of the size of Seggieden. Furthermore, lying very close to the great houses and quite separate from the landscaped park, the flower gardens remained. Indeed, these were formal flower gardens, designed, as likely as not, by the same Humphry Repton or other modifier of nature who had created the park. So we should really look to the smaller properties of the less lavishly landed gentry of the time for the foundations of what was to follow. For there, in the absence of a landscaped park, or even of any park at all, most gardens still had geometrically patterned beds and formal parterres. Apart from the fruit and vegetables to feed the household, they were still, in essence, flower gardens.

This was the background to the early nineteenth century and the Victorian garden itself. Here we must be careful with our terminology, for while, strictly speaking, the Victorian age spanned the sixty-three years of Victoria's reign from 1837 to 1901, important developments affecting what we now call Victorian gardening had clearly begun years earlier. Equally, other developments of even greater importance for the modern garden began right at the end of the reign and were to continue long after the Queen herself was dead and buried. Seggieden itself was at its height in the 1880s and 1890s.

ROBERT FORTUNE

Five years after Victoria's coronation in 1837 came a political agreement that for botany and horticulture was arguably the most important ever signed. The Treaty of Nanking and the end of the Chinese Opium War in 1842 allowed Britain for the first time the right of entry to the interior of China. The Horticultural Society in London was not slow off the mark to capitalize on this, and in the following year they dispatched the young Scotsman, Robert Fortune, with a collection of Wardian cases (see page 34) to bring back certain plants which were known to be growing in Chinese gardens. Fortune spent three years in China and returned not only with the required plants and the art of chrysanthemum growing but also with an urge to return to the Far East once more.

During the succeeding years, Fortune lived dangerously but survived to learn the Chinese secret of tea growing and obtained sufficient plants to establish the tea industries both of India and Ceylon. His journeys into the remoter areas of China were limited and explorers like George Forrest and Ernest Wilson later in the century were far more successful in collecting wild as opposed to already cultivated species. But Fortune had been the first into China, the first to use and demonstrate the value of the Wardian case, and had in a very real sense been the trailblazer for the enrichment of Western gardens.

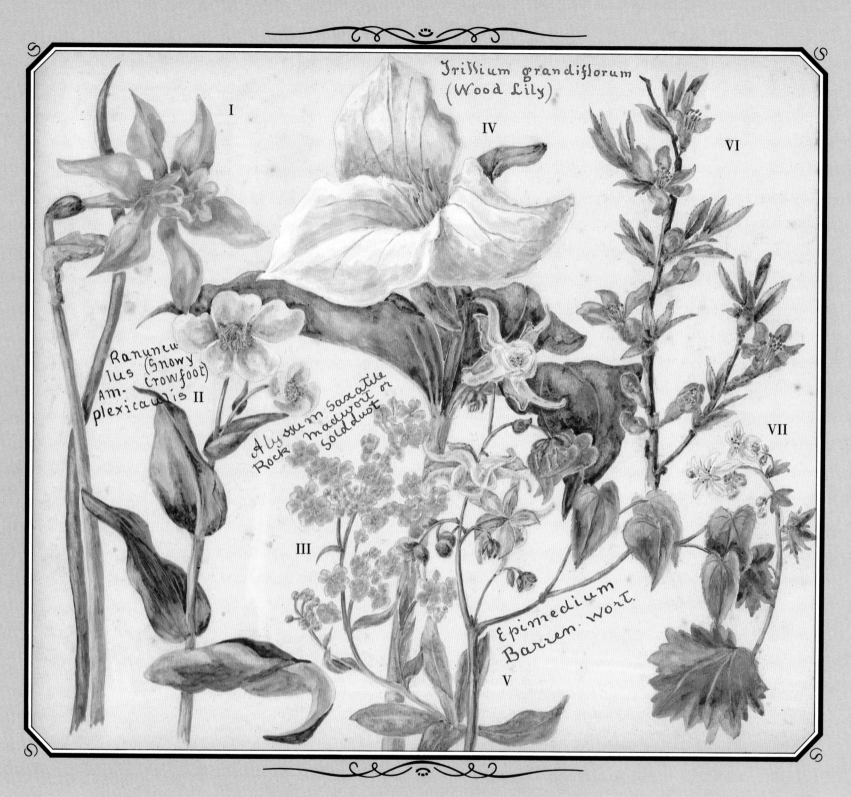

Trillium grandiflorum
(Wood Lily)

Ranunculus (Snowy crowfoot) Amplexicaulis

Alyssum saxatile Rock madwort or Golddust

Epimedium Barren-wort.

I   II   III   IV   V   VI   VII

I *Narcissus* sp. · Narcissus   **II** *Ranunculus amplexicaulis*
III *Alyssum saxatile* · Golden alyssum   **IV** *Trillium grandiflorum* · Wood lily
V *Epimedium* sp. · Barrenwort   **VI** *Prunus* sp. · probably Peach
VII *Anemone* sp.(?)

Trollius Napellifolius
(Globe Flower)
I

Fritillaria-
Meleagris. (Snakeshead)
(Fritillary)

III

II
Saxifraga
wallacei

I *Trollius europaeus* · Globe flower   II *Saxifraga wallacei*
III *Fritillaria meleagris* · Snake's head fritillary

'BEDS' AND 'BORDERS'

To my mind, the two key words in Victorian flower gardening (words which form pivots around which much of the subject matter of this book rotates) are 'bed' and 'border', in the sense defined by William Cobbett in his 'English Gardener' of 1828. He described a bed as a planting predominantly of one type of flower, whereas a border contains a mixture, often a very great mixture. It was the bed that was to dominate the first few decades, and a form of the border, the latter few. However, this is not to say, as is sometimes assumed, that mixed planting of flowers was a late nineteenth-century invention. There have always been times and gardens when mixed plantings have been made. Even in the Tudor garden, different types of flower could be found intermingled, and certainly there were mixed borders at the start of the Victorian period. But, in large measure, the earlier mixtures were mixtures of annuals, whereas the mixed border that

came to such pre-eminence in the later years of Victoria's reign was the herbaceous border composed largely of perennials. And even that, as I shall be explaining later, was far from a late nineteenth-century discovery,

The flower bed or the flower border known to Cobbett would have contained a very different range of flowers from those that have later come to be associated with the archetypal Victorian flower garden. The main reason for this was the fall in the price of glass. For while Cobbett would have seen annuals, they would have been predominantly hardy annuals (or biennials)) such as wallflowers, sweet williams, convolvulus, hawkweeds and mignonette, along with tulips, hyacinths, ranunculus and other bulbous and tuberous plants. Almost all had a short flowering season.

The wider availability of greenhouses and cold frames stimulated the rise in importance of the half-hardy annual. Think of the nearest thing in Britain we still have to a Victorian flower bed

An archetypal English cottage garden at Maltingley, Hampshire around the turn of the century.

today, the municipal flower garden, and you will have a vision of pelargoniums, tagetes, petunias, perhaps fuchsias, verbenas, salvia, ageratum, lobelia and *Begonia semperflorens*. Almost none of these was available before about 1820, and none could be raised other than by the very rich with their glasshouses for another twenty years. But as the century progressed, they were joined by a whole host of other half-hardy bedding plants that have since fallen from favour. How many gardeners today can even describe, let alone grow alonsoas, alternantheras, bouvardias, calandrinias, cacalias, hebenstreitias, iresines, madias and perillas? Those who do know them will realize that some are foliage plants, and the importance accorded to leaf colour in creating the patterns of what came to be known towards the end of the century as carpet bedding (in which the flower beds copied the patterns on real carpets and wallpapers) was enormous.

VARIETY AND INFORMALITY

Gradually, and to some degree independently, more and more of the mid-Victorian gardeners came to rebel against the formal bedding style; often as much for economic and logistic as aesthetic reasons. Inspired by what Kent, Brown and Repton had done for the landscape, and ever full of admiration for the traditional English cottage garden, they began to bring elements of the cottage garden to the fore. They concentrated, in particular, on the elements that blended a range of hardy herbaceous perennials to produce mixed borders giving colour not just for a few weeks but in sequence for months (without the intervention of replanting) and that would mature over a period of years. The grand master of this approach was William Robinson, whose 'English Flower Garden', published in 1883, synthesizes many of these principles. It has of late become fashionable in some quarters to denigrate Robinson's contribution, dubbing him merely a journalist and popularizer of others' ideas. This is scarcely fair,

for whereas Robinson and his remarkable contemporary Gertrude Jekyll did not invent, and never claimed to have invented, the herbaceous border, they did at least as much to spread the message as Shirley Hibberd, William Morris, John Ruskin and the other driving forces of gardening and style in Britain at the time. And they were as willing as anyone to give credit to the numerous, often unknown and unsung head gardeners up and down the land whose only misfortune was that their skills lay solely with the trowel and the propagating bench, not the English language. There were certainly herbaceous borders in existence as early as the 1840s (and, of course, herbaceous perennials in plenty, especially in cottage gardens, for longer still), but without the combined thunder of Robinson's pen and Jekyll's drawing board, they could now be as much a part of history as the Tudor knot.

Thus, when, around 1890, Alice Drummond-Hay painted the flowers at Seggieden, her home environment was that of a typical small country house and garden of the time. It was a garden containing both formal and informal elements, a blend of the hardy perennial and the half-hardy bedding annual, flowers for admiring *en masse* and *in situ*, and flowers for cutting. There were ample numbers, too, of roses and other flowering shrubs and of ornamental trees; together, of course, with vegetables and fruit, a walled garden, beds, borders, parterres, shrubberies and woodland walks, vineries, cold frames, propagating houses and hot beds. At that period, perhaps for the last time in gardening and social history, it was possible, in any one of hundreds of comparable gardens up and down the land, to see encapsulated in a relatively small area so many of the multifarious elements that had contributed to British gardening over the centuries. Although few of us today have the scope, labour resources or money to re-create a Seggieden, many elements in the late Victorian flower garden which it exemplified are certainly worthy of being reproduced.

Sutton's catalogue of around 1885, advertised here, was like many other catalogues of the time, more of a textbook than merely a list of varieties.

CHAPTER III

GARDENING TECHNIQUES-THEN AND NOW

GARDENS DO NOT, of course, create themselves. They are the products of man's understanding of nature, of his intelligence and resourcefulness, and also of his ingenuity and hard labour. The gardener must have a grasp of certain basic principles of seed sowing and plant raising, of propagating, feeding and watering, of composts, manures and fertilizers and of pest and disease control. Over the past twenty or thirty years, many such facets of a gardener's life have been made simpler and, in recreating a Victorian-style garden today, I can see no justification in resorting to outmoded or inferior horticultural principles. Nonetheless, a grasp of the procedures that would have been employed one hundred or more years ago will certainly help you to appreciate the end product that the Victorian gardener achieved. And there are certainly some unashamedly late twentieth-century inventions that would jar alarmingly in an authentic period piece.

RAISING FROM SEED

Much of gardening starts with seeds, and we now take for granted the mail order or over-the-counter purchase of seeds of high quality and reliable germination, and in a seemingly good range of varieties. The range today is, in fact, probably larger than that available in the nine-teenth century although smaller than that on offer in early twentieth-century Britain.

There was a strong feeling, often promoted in magazines of the period (who were looking, perhaps, to their advertising revenue) that the Victorian gardener should purchase his seeds from 'reputable seedsmen' rather than collect his own from the garden. In general, this is still good advice; indeed, the advent of the F_1 hybrid (whose progeny are a useless hotch potch) has rendered it even more so.

Nonetheless, it is not often appreciated how widespread was the nineteenth-century trade in Britain in mail order plants. Then as now, there were many named varieties of garden flowers that did not come true from seed and could only be propagated by cuttings. And having no retail outlet comparable with the garden centre, anyone not within easy reach of a nursery had to rely on this method of purchase. Advertisements abounded in the press, and it was not only commercial nurseries that supplied the plants. Many of the advertisements emanated from private addresses; and a disproportionately large number from vicarages.

Today, flower seeds are sown in one of two main ways: either in spring and, occasionally, in autumn, directly into their flowering positions in the garden (the normal practice with hardy annuals); or into a proprietary seedling mixture

Mertensia virginica (Virginian Cowslip) I

Kalmia III

Gaultheria shallon II

Aquilegea canadensis (Canadian Columbine) IV

Aquilegea Chrysantha — (Golden Columbine) V

VI Aquilegea glandulosa Columbine (Altaian Mountain)

I *Mertensia virginica* · Virginian cowslip   **II** *Gaultheria shallon* · Shallon

III *Kalmia latifolia*   **IV** *Aquilegia canadensis* · Columbine

V *Aquilegia chrysantha* · Columbine   **VI** *Aquilegia glandulosa* · Columbine

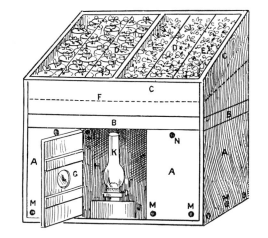

Many Victorian propagating cases relied on the bain-marie principle, in which a lamp (annotated as 'K' in this drawing) heated a water tank (B) above which the potted seedlings (E) were plunged in beds of coconut fibre.

a transparent plastic cover and, increasingly, with a small electric thermostatically controlled heating element as well.

Times have changed: the Victorian gardener had no plastic, little electricity, and no specially prepared seedling mixture. He would use a blend of loam, well-rotted leaf mould (or 'leaf soil' as it was known) and sand, in proportions suggested by the gardener's experience or by his reference book. The nineteenth-century soil-based mixture had no sterilized components, so the danger of fungus-caused damping off occurring among the seedlings was high. Then, the only protection against it was to pay assiduous attention to ventilation (no bad maxim, even now) and, if all else failed, to drench the compost with copper-containing fungicides known as Bordeaux or Burgundy mixtures. In a large, heated greenhouse, sulphur might have been painted onto the heating pipes so that it vaporized and acted as a fungicidal fumigant.

in some form of propagator. The latter method is the normal procedure with half-hardy annuals or with hardy types if they are to give the earliest flowering and strongest plants. The seedling medium is either a soil-less, peat-based blend with a carefully regulated artificial fertilizer content, or a special soil-based preparation. The propagator could range from a plastic pot covered with a plastic bag to a plastic seed tray (flat) with

The nineteenth-century propagator or propagating case, used both for seeds and cuttings, was

A CUTTING EDGE

If I had to name the garden hand-tool most taken for granted today and yet the one which the amateur gardener would be most at a loss without, I think that the one-hand pruner or secateur would have to take the award. Most amateur gardeners today, even if they possess a gardening knife, use it almost exclusively for cutting string and would be quite at a loss to know how to use it for pruning. Yet although the basic two-blade or scissor-action principle has been known for centuries, its adaptation to a pruning tool was very much a nineteenth-century creation. And what a weird and wonderful selection was produced, many of them quite astonishingly large and heavy – indicative of large, strong, nineteenth-century hands.

Improvements in metal technology and the ability to produce a durable, sharp cutting edge in stainless steel have meant that the modern lightweight scissor-action or by-pass secateur is a very precise implement indeed. And it has now been joined by

the single-handed, single-bladed anvil-action pruner, in which the blade is forced against a flat, anvil surface. Nonetheless, even today there are those professional and serious amateur gardeners who spurn such appliances, believing that a razor-sharp pruning knife in skilled hands is without equal. But let it not be forgotten that in unskilled hands, it can become an amputation instrument.

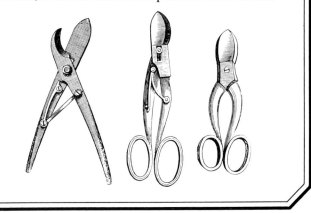

as varied as it was ingenious. One common example operated on the *bain-marie* principle: a small oil lamp heated a bath of water above which the germinating or rooting bed was fixed. A simpler system for rooting cuttings comprised a double plant pot, one inside the other, with soil between the two and with watering performed through the centre pot. A bell jar over the whole maintained a moist environment. Most frequently, the gardener with heating pipes in his greenhouse would stand his shallow wooden seed boxes or terra cotta seed pans, covered with glass sheet, over the pipes. But just as the gardener today, with no such heating and even with no greenhouse, may make good use of a warm indoor cupboard to see his seedlings to the stage of emerging through the mixture (when they must swiftly be transferred to the light), so the late Victorian gardener made use of the cupboards either side of the kitchen range where the required temperature of about 18°C (65°F) could be readily maintained.

Electricity was a latecomer to amateur gardening and had barely appeared by the close of the Victorian period although, in passing, reference must be made to the curious phenomenon of electro-horticulture which gained a following at the time. It was believed that growing plants in soil exposed to a continuous electric current improved their growth, and ingenious if not bizarre contrivances were erected in which the seedling container became in effect an electric cell.

GREENHOUSES AND FRAMES

The wealthier gardener in Victorian times would, of course, have had the luxury of a greenhouse, usually built of wood, although the grander structures were of metal (cast iron, not today's aluminium) and commonly ornate. Usually, they were painted not white, but green. In the smaller garden, the greenhouse shape would not be recognizably different from many today – rectangular with a span roof and vertical sides. The hemispherical shape that actually has the most efficient light-collecting qualities, which has recently been offered as a high-priced aluminium novelty, is not

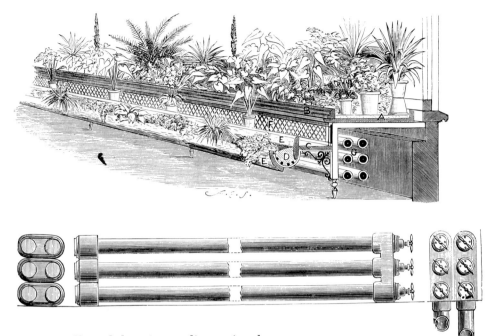

novel at all and has its pedigree in the once-popular nineteenth-century curvilinear house.

The commonest, least efficient and most uncontrollable modern greenhouse heating system is the paraffin (kerosene) burner; the best is the thermostatically controlled electric fan or radiant heater. The Victorians, however, heated their greenhouses by means of a small coal-fired boiler, usually sited in a house adjacent to the main structure, from which hot water pipes ran beneath the staging. The start to every gardener's day in

A typically ornate Victorian *greenhouse staging, heated in this instance by hot water using 'Ormson's Divisional Heating Apparatus'.*

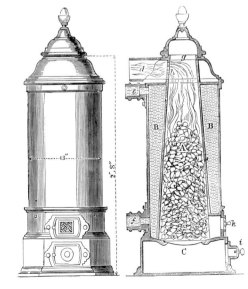

The ultimate source of greenhouse heat in almost every case was a coal-fired boiler, this particular model being portable – although presumably only when cold.

I *Polemonium coeruleum* · Jacob's ladder
II *Kerria japonica* · Jew's mallow
III *Prunus dulcis (= Amygdalis)* · Almond   **IV** *Rhododendron* sp.
V Unidentified

I *Geum coccineum* · Avens II *Narcissus poeticus* III *Viola* sp. · Pansy
IV *Fritillaria imperialis* · Crown imperial V *Trillium erectum*
VI *Lunaria biennis* · Honesty

winter was to rake out the ash-pan and stoke the boiler. Gradually, small versions were manufactured especially for amateur use. It is doubtful, however, if Alice Drummond-Hay ever saw the 'Stourbridge Heating Apparatus', complete with 18 feet of 4 inch pipe, advertised in 1892 for supply and delivery free to the nearest railway station for £4, for the offer of this particular model was restricted to England and Wales.

The cold frame of today, an indispensable aid to hardening off bedding plants before planting them in the open garden, is perhaps the gardening apparatus that the nineteenth-century gardener would most readily recognize for it has changed little. Nowadays, however, like the modern greenhouse, its framework is most commonly of aluminium, not wood, whereas the cloche, that most misunderstood and underused of gardening aids, has changed beyond recognition. In the flower garden, its greatest (but least appreciated) asset is its ability to pre-warm the soil before sowing or planting, but the characteristic glass Victorian bell cloche is now a valued collector's item. A modern alternative is equally efficient, although glass is much to be preferred to translucent plastic sheet which, while causing the interior to heat up more quickly, allows it to cool down more quickly too.

PLANTING OUT

For raising plants, the modern plastic pot offers a cheap and more durable alternative to the traditional terra cotta, with which the Victorian gardener would have been familiar. However, the plastic pot does have its drawbacks for, being non-porous, it may allow the internal atmosphere to become stagnant and the growing medium waterlogged. When large pots are used outdoors for semi-permanent plantings, more traditional styles must, of course, be used but bear in mind the following points. Some modern terra cotta pots are neither very porous (being externally glazed) nor frost-resistant, so check these features with suppliers and manufacturers. Ornamental pots made from other materials now abound and, although natural stone is prohibitively expensive, good and barely indistinguishable substitutes exist, based on reconstituted stone or concrete. Check the frost tolerance of these too, and make sure that no chemical hardener has been used that would prove toxic to plants until the pots are thoroughly weathered.

AUTHENTIC TOUCHES

Once plants are established in the garden, the peripheral matters become visually important if a modern garden is to be authentically similar to its Victorian counterpart. For plant support, there really can be no substitute for wood, either in the shape of bundles of twigs (used in preference to the modern metal contraptions for herbaceous perennials), or stakes, be they of bamboo cane, or sawn oak or chestnut for trees and shrubs. For tying herbaceous plants, there is no alternative, either visually or functionally, to jute twine or raffia, although in the earlier part of the nineteenth

A lean-to greenhouse for cucumbers, heated by hot water circulating through slate tanks.

A scene typical of almost any country house garden in the middle of the nineteenth century; note the remarkably heavy wheelbarrow, the sliding lights on the cold frame and the greenhouse chimney.

'An Amateur Gardener' *in 1885, sowing seeds from a packet.*

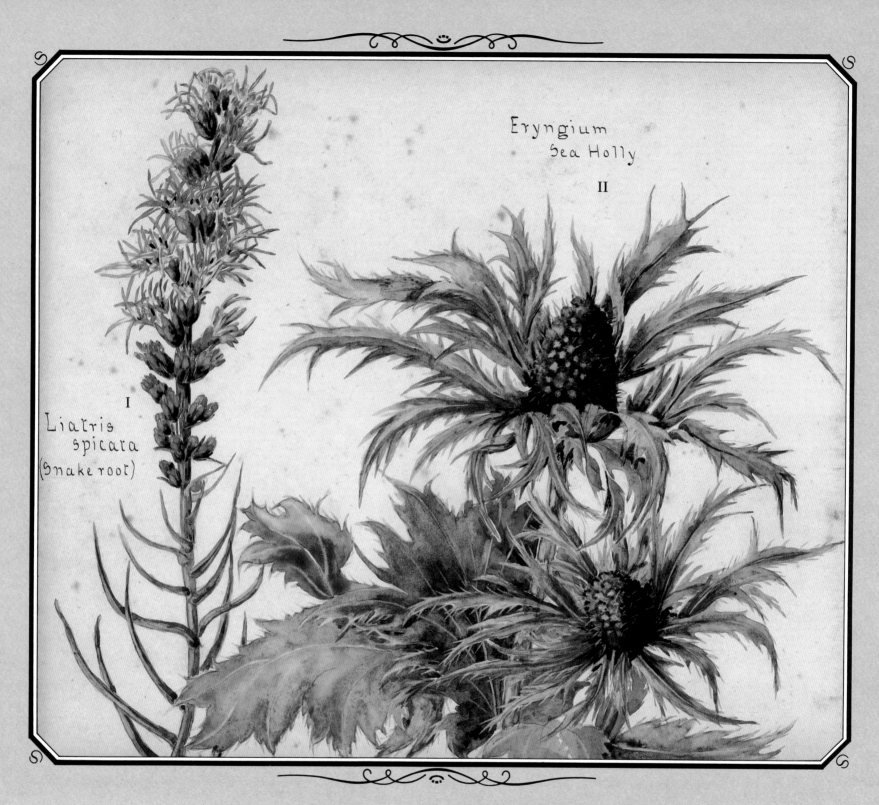

Eryngium
Sea Holly

II

I

Liatris
spicara
(Snake root)

I *Liatris spicaria* · Snake root **II** *Eryngium maritimum* · Sea holly

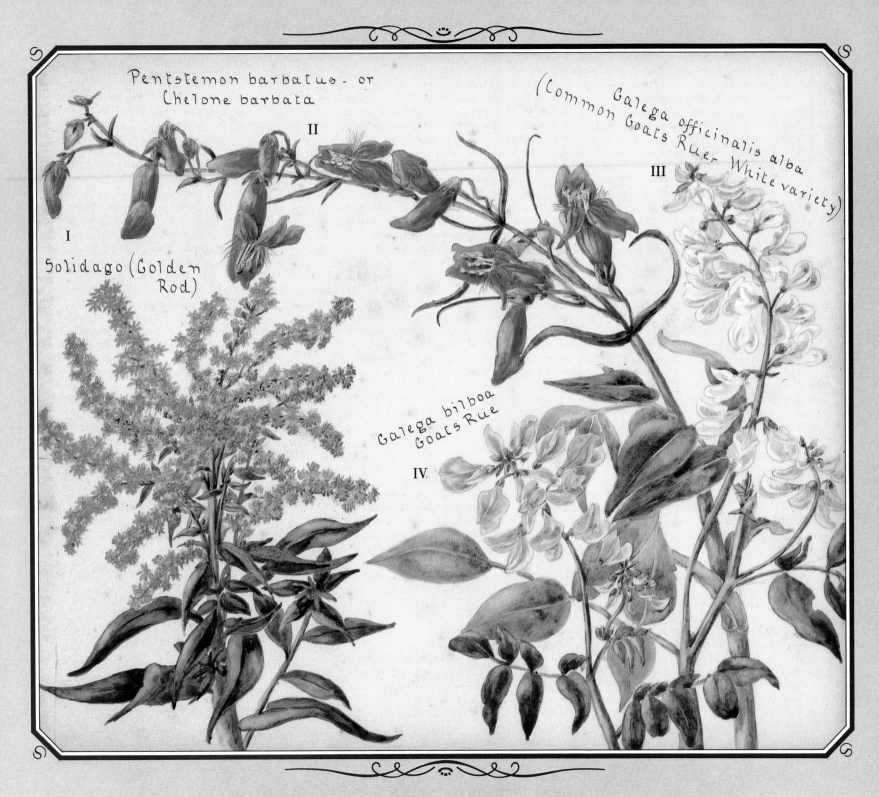

Pentstemon barbatus - or
Chelone barbata

Galega officinalis alba
(Common Goats Rue - White variety)

II

III

I

Solidago (Golden
Rod)

Galega bilboa
Goats Rue

IV

I *Solidago* sp. · Golden rod   II *Penstemon (= Chelone) barbatus*
III *Galega officinalis* · Goat's rue   IV *Galega officinalis* · Goat's rue

Patent metal plant labels – these could be inscribed with ordinary ink and yet would remain legible 'even after years of exposure'.

century pliable willow shoots were used to secure trees and shrubs either to stakes or to walls or other supports. Plastic-coated wire is acceptable for climbers provided the ties are checked once a year to avoid any unnecessary constriction. Plastic must be admissable, too, in the modern belt-style tree tie which expands as the tree grows and minimizes the likelihood of the stem being damaged by constriction. To secure the tying wire, and anchor a robust climber to a wall, a hardwood peg (or possibly a stout modern plastic or fibre wall-plug and iron vine eye) is still to my mind invaluable, although for more pliable shoots like those of clematis, the lead-headed nail is an attractive if expensive alternative.

Once planted, the new shrub, tree, herbaceous perennial or bed of annuals required a label. Today, the modern plastic label is wholly inappropriate (and looks very ugly) yet there is no acceptable and inexpensive alternative for mass use, although fairly low-priced zinc-coated types are much to be preferred for semi-permanent positions. Nonetheless, for a showpiece Victorian-style garden, a few original or reproduction labels of the period would put a stamp on its authenticity. And what variety there was: from ephemeral hardwood to perennial ceramic or, perhaps commonest of all, cast zinc. Recipes for manufacturing indelible ink for use on zinc labels were commonly published in the gardening literature. Most beautiful of all, although well nigh unobtainable now, was the so-called crystal weatherproof label, comprising waxed paper sealed within some glass container, usually a small tube, with a tie for attaching it to trees or shrubs.

FEEDING

The feeding of growing and mature plants has become simplicity itself and just as the modern ranges of seed sowing and potting mixtures have

THE WARDIAN CASE

No one gardens for very long before discovering that plants do not take kindly to a life in which their roots are denied soil. Even with present-day high-speed travel, cherished cuttings carried to distant relatives are as likely as not to arrive shrivelled and worthless. In the nineteenth century, the difficulties were compounded ten thousand times as explorers attempted to bring back tender plants on their long sea voyages. Other than with very resilient woody material (and, of course, seeds), the task was almost hopeless.

Enter Dr Nathaniel Bagshaw Ward of London who began a series of experiments with miniature, sealed greenhouses complete with moist soil. Plants enclosed in these containers clearly could survive for months if not years as the water given off by their leaves condensed on the glass and was returned to the soil. During the 1830s, Ward sent such a case of plants to Australia. They survived; and so did Australian species dispatched by return. Plant movement around the world was thus revolutionized and Robert Fortune on his journeys into China

became the first of many plant collectors to use the technique. Today, high-speed air travel has rendered the Wardian case obsolete, although the principle remains in many modern homes in the shape of sealed bottle gardens and terraria.

replaced the 'muck and mystery' mixtures, so pre-packed fertilizers have replaced what might most charitably be called the individuality of the Victorian equivalents. Now, as then, both artificial and so-called organic fertilizers were obtainable and it is interesting to realize that the varied opinions of their respective merits, currently the source of so much gardening controversy, are by no means a modern phenomenon. The relative pros and cons of the 'traditional' products and the 'modern' manufactured fertilizers filled much column space on the correspondence pages of the gardening journals of the nineteenth century, just as they do today. While solid manures, emanating from cow, horse or pig, were used extensively both as soil amendment and plant food, great store was placed on liquid extracts of natural animal manure, blended in various ways. The compost heap or *omnium gatherum* was given as much prominence in the garden then as it should now be given, but it is with solid fertilizers, rather than bulky organic materials, that the greatest changes and advances in plant feeding have been made. Among the organic products once popular were the raw guanos (seabird droppings) of which the best were imported from Africa. Among so-called straight fertilizers to be found in almost every Victorian potting shed were common salt, gas-liquor (a mixture of ammonium salts) and a very wide range of now-forgotten potassium and sodium compounds.

But a short range of proprietary blended mixtures will satisfy virtually all of the modern gardener's needs and I would commend the following list: a balanced general solid fertilizer (either an artificial blend or the organically based Blood, Fish and Bone), a balanced liquid fertilizer for general feeding during the growing season, a liquid tomato fertilizer containing a high proportion of potash for swift results on flowering plants, two lawn fertilizers (one high in nitrogen for spring and summer and one high in phosphate for autumn use) and bone meal as a planting treatment to supply a source of slow-release phosphate to aid root development.

PEST AND DISEASE CONTROL

Some comments on the relative problems, then and now, of keeping various types of flower gardens free from pests and diseases are made in subsequent chapters but the equipment used to apply the remedies deserves a mention. Today, a garden sprayer will almost invariably be of plastic and incorporate a small graduated reservoir within which the pesticide is diluted. For the Victorians, the sprayer was usually a more or less complex brass syringe used with an open bucket of spray-strength mixture. Such old sprayers still turn up in antique shops and, although scarcely to be recommended for their original purpose, they do make splendid ornaments when polished and hung on the potting shed wall.

'The best remedy.' Pest control has always been a serious matter.

CHAPTER IV

THE FRAMEWORK OF THE VICTORIAN GARDEN

Inventiveness *in providing supports for climbing plants almost knew no bounds.*

Fencing *in a Chinese influenced ornate pattern.*

THERE IS MUCH more to a garden than its plants, and it is indeed the non-living framework that best conveys an immediate overall impression of time, period and style. So before you even sow your first seed or introduce your first plant, you should already have gone some way towards giving your garden its unmistakably Victorian stamp.

In Victorian times, just as now, there was no right and wrong way to organize the entire garden, no indisputably correct place to site the fruit, vegetables and various ornamental areas. But the nineteenth-century garden owner, usually employing at least one gardener and/or labourer to carry the baskets or wheel the barrows, could afford to tuck the walled vegetable and fruit garden some distance away from the eyes of the family and the house guests who gazed through the drawing room windows. It makes a great deal more sense today to ensure that at least the herbs and the salad vegetables are within easy picking distance of the kitchen. Nonetheless, even if there is no strict blueprint to follow, it will be useful to draw up an overall plan of the area to be used for the period re-creation, be it a single flower bed, a rose garden, a series of herbaceous borders, or simply a selection of appropriately planted pots in a courtyard.

In this chapter I shall consider the framework of the garden, which encompasses the non-living materials of the boundary fence or wall, paths, courtyards and terraces, path and bed edgings, seats and other furniture, ornaments and statuary. There are living structural features to consider as well — the lawn, of course, which will be discussed here, and the so-called architectural plants — the hedges and the topiary — which are described in Chapter VIII.

FENCES AND WALLS

One of the most characteristic and structurally important features of the nineteenth-century garden — cast iron boundary railings — is, unfortunately, one of the most expensive to provide today. In Britain, countless miles of old railings disappeared into the armaments factories of the Second World War and were never replaced; and although it would be unrealistic nowadays to attempt to define any other than the very smallest garden entirely with railings, it may be possible to obtain relatively short lengths and use them

July Gold, *Abbeyleix, Ireland, by Ernest Arthur Rowe.*

around a particular feature. Simpler and cheaper than rails, and perhaps the best overall choice for the modern-day Victorian garden, is the picket fence, made from vertical, pointed timber boards, spaced a few inches apart and nailed to two horizontal lengths. Almost invariably, nineteenth-century picket fencing was painted white, and modern outdoor paints which allow the timber to 'breathe' and are much more resistant than traditional types to cracking and peeling, are strongly recommended. In a rural house or cottage garden, rustic timber fencing, about one metre (3 feet) high, is also acceptably in keeping, although modern prefabricated fencing panels of overlapping or interwoven softwoods would be quite out of character. Gates, of course, should match as far as possible the fencing style.

It is unlikely that many gardeners today would go to the trouble or, more pertinently, to the expense of building a replica Victorian garden wall, either of brick or stone. For those who would, or more especially for those who already have an old wall and wish to restore it, one or two points should be borne in mind. Victorian bricks varied widely in type and size, and were manufactured in a considerable range of colours. It is almost impossible to match any modern brick satisfactorily with old weathered bricks, and two

A very functional and robust oak-pale fence in a Victorian garden. Today, the cost would be prohibitive.

Every garden must have its paths and most should also have some form of terrace, courtyard or other paved area; but before embarking on construction, one factor, the cost, must be borne very carefully in mind. The total area covered even by a fairly modest path is considerable, and many of the paving materials used in the nineteenth century, or their modern replicas, are now very expensive, both to purchase and to have laid expertly. It is perhaps easiest to consider only three of the numerous possibilities for the Victorian garden – brick, stone and gravel – and to use them as resources allow. Bricks are the most costly, most difficult to lay, but most appropriate for the town garden. They should preferably be bedded on a concrete or mortar base and can be arranged in a wide variety of pleasing patterns, virtually all faithful to the nineteenth century; of these the herringbone perhaps has the greatest

options, therefore, are open. Either existing but flawed old bricks in the wall may be turned, to make use of their better, inner face, or bricks of comparable age and pattern must be obtained from a demolished local property. A builder experienced in these matters will be an invaluable help, for he can advise also on appropriate and sympathetic methods of pointing and capping.

Few types of paving can match the beauty and appeal of natural stone although its cost today necessitates a reconstituted stone alternative.

appeal. It is important to remember that bricks used for paths are subject to a great deal of wear and tear and weathering; discarded building bricks are unlikely to be sufficiently durable and may crumble after a few severe frosts. For preference, use old engineering bricks, but new bricks or modern brick paviours are possible alternatives.

Whereas natural York or other paving stone, either new or secondhand, is often extraordinarily expensive, there are modern reconstituted stone equivalents that look almost as attractive. They are also easier to lay than natural stone because, being of uniform thickness, they can be bedded onto a concrete base. Natural stones should be laid onto a hardcore base covered by a layer of sand, each individual stone being cemented beneath and then pushed into the sand to an appropriate depth in order to give a level top surface.

Although inappropriate for the authentic rural nineteenth-century garden, mention must be made of the more ornate path and terrace surfaces that became popular, especially in town gardens, towards the end of the Victorian period. The style that we now call crazy paving was perhaps the most restrained of these, but complex and sometimes bizarre and almost pictorial arrangements were produced also from combinations of stone, brick, tiles, cobbles and other materials.

Of all path materials, however, the cheapest and easiest to lay is undoubtedly gravel, which can, of course, be used for larger areas as well. In one form or another, gravel has been used in gardens for centuries and is wholly appropriate for the Victorian garden, in urban or rural situations. Cheapest of all is the small, rounded type generally called pea gravel. Its biggest drawback is the need for regular raking and its liability to be moved around by cars when used on a driveway; this was much less of a problem when only Victorian carriage wheels were involved. More expensive but more stable, and generally requiring less raking, are various types of crushed stone.

Two general considerations for all types of gravelled areas are the need to combat weed growth and to prevent the gravel itself from wandering

onto beds and borders. The former problem was combated in the nineteenth century by hand weeding or, later, by the use of salt or carbolic acid at the rate of 1 oz per gallon. It can be dealt with very satisfactorily today by one of the many specific path weedkillers. But it is in the means used to confine the gravel by some form of path edging that much nineteenth-century flavour can be brought to the garden as a whole. Metallic-finished, hard terra cotta path edgings with ornate tops in rope-like or other patterns were produced by the thousand in the second half of the century. Sadly, only a small proportion of the originals survive but several manufacturers produce excellent modern replicas. Terra cotta would prove very costly for edging long gravel paths, and the simplest and cheapest solution, quite appropriate to a Victorian setting, is wood. Lengths of half-round softwood treated with a modern timber preservative and held in place with hardwood pegs will last for many years.

Most gardens will have at least a few steps and, indeed, will need at least a few to introduce desirable changes of level. Steps for the formal garden should ideally be of stone or reconstituted stone, preferably with matching stone balustrade or cast-

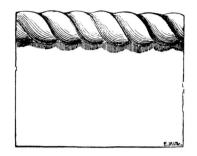

Terra cotta rope-top path edgings are especially appropriate for the Victorian town garden.

Steps are invaluable where levels change, but few modern gardeners could hope to match these Victorian originals from an 1866 book by John Hughes illustrating 'the architectural embellishment of gardens'.

Tiarella cordifolia
(The Foam Flower)

Dicentra Spectabilis
(Bleeding Heart)

II

I

III

I *Tiarella cordifolia* · Foam flower   **II** *Dicentra spectabilis* · Bleeding heart
III *Rhododendron* sp.

I *Lychnis sylvestris* · Campion   II *Dryas octopetala* · Mountain avens
III *Phlox nivalis*   IV *Dodecatheon maedia* · Shooting star

Even a simple series of stone steps can add enormous interest to a garden and provide extra areas on which to place containers.

gave so much impetus to their further use (both for ornament and for croquet and other games) as the invention that was first wheeled out in the early 1830s, the cylinder mower. This was based on a design by a textile engineer named Edwin Budding and almost overnight replaced the centuries-old scythe and besom. Budding's basic design of the small pushed (or, in the nineteenth century, sometimes pulled) cylinder mower has remained virtually unchanged since, although in recent years it has been almost entirely supplanted for small gardens by the electric rotary. Although powered mowers did not appear, at least in amateurs' gardens, until the present century, most garden owners today have a petrol or electric machine. In re-creating an authentic feel to the garden, it should nonetheless be remembered that, because the Victorian garden was cut by a cylinder mower, it would have had the appealing striped appearance that has all but vanished where cutting is done with a rotary. Probably the ideal machine for the small Victorian-style lawn garden today is one of the most recent advents to the lawnmower market, the small, electrically powered cylinder mower. Grass edging was performed then, as almost invariably now, with shears and edging knives.

The nineteenth-century garden used grass in far more intricate ways than the conventional and fairly regular lawn patterns that we have today, and many complex Victorian bedding schemes included a turfed component. Indeed, in order to reconstruct some of the more complex bedding patterns on a small scale, it may be necessary to cut the grassed areas with shears, because the special narrow Victorian border mower, formerly

iron railings, but these can be costly to construct. Bricks offer a less expensive alternative, although even here the cost may prove prohibitive. For long flights, rustic wooden steps with strong wooden risers held in place with stout pegs may be the only feasible proposition.

LAWNS

And so to perhaps the most important of the living structural features – the lawn. Lawns, or at least areas of cut grass, have been important garden features at least since medieval times. But nothing

Green's Mowing Machine of the 1880s was little different in its overall design from Budding's original of fifty years earlier.

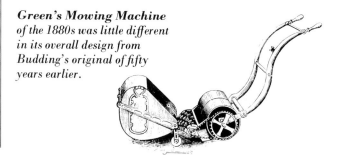

PAXTON, CHATSWORTH AND *VICTORIA REGIA*

If one plant can be said to sum up the botanical and horticultural excitement of the Victorian age, it is the great water lily named after the Queen herself – *Victoria regia*. Couple this amazing plant's discovery with the character of Joseph Paxton who designed the greatest symbol of nineteenth-century technology, the Crystal Palace of the Great Exhibition held in 1851, and add too what is arguably the greatest of English country houses, Chatsworth in Derbyshire, and you have a compelling story indeed.

Victoria regia has leaves 2 metres (6 feet) across and when it was discovered in British Guiana in the Queen's coronation year, there could be only one ambition – seeds must be sent to England and this amazing plant must be persuaded to grow and flower.

Many gardeners tried but many failed. If success was to come, it was almost inevitable that it should do so at the hands of Joseph Paxton, gardener to the 6th Duke of Devonshire. Paxton had a way with glass and built at Chatsworth a Great Conservatory, at the time the largest glasshouse in the world. In his lily house, Paxton persuaded the giant lily to grow and eventually, in 1849, it flowered. The curiously efficient ribbed structure of the vast leaves, so strong that they supported the weight of Paxton's daughter, led to further fame. For Paxton adopted a similar pattern for the iron work of the greatest of all glass buildings, the Crystal Palace, which he was subsequently invited to build. Sadly, Paxton's glass palaces have gone, but *Victoria regia* survives to be admired in great botanic gardens the world over.

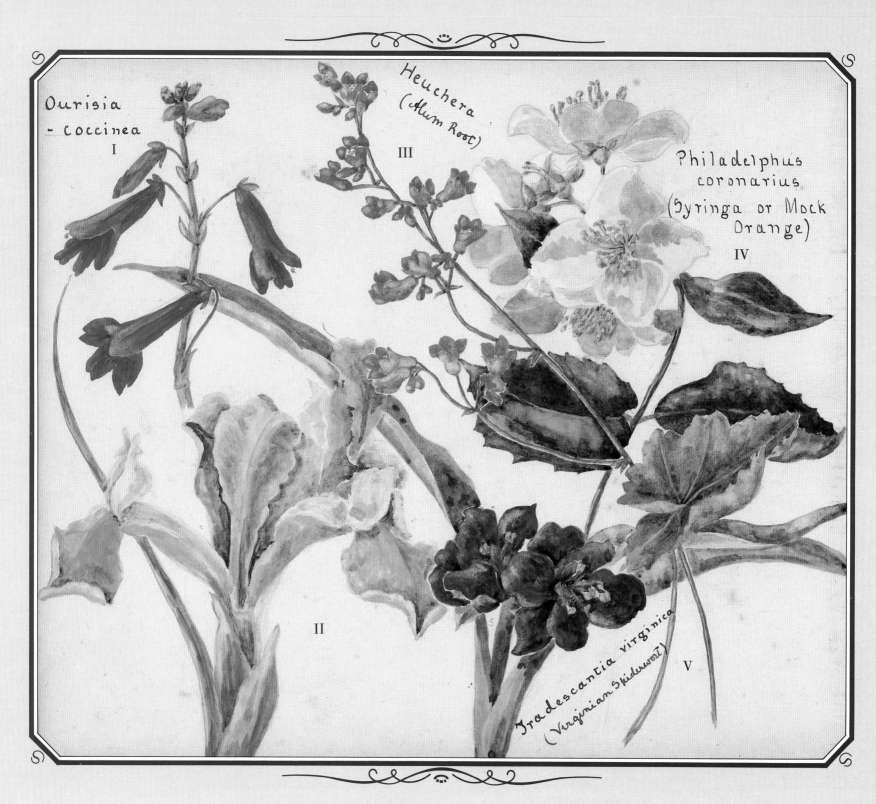

Ourisia
- coccinea
I

Heuchera
(Alum Root)
III

Philadelphus
coronarius
(Syringa or Mock
Orange)
IV

II

Tradescantia virginica
(Virginian Spiderwort)
V

I *Ourisia coccinea*   II *Iris* sp.   III *Heuchera* sp. · Alum root
IV *Philadelphus coronarius* · Mock orange   V *Tradescantia virginiana*

Buddlea globosa
(Round-headed Budlea)

I

Gaillardia

III

II
Pyrethrum
Caucasian

IV
Lathyrus grandflorus
(Everlasting Pea)

I *Buddleia globosa*   II *Tanacetum coccineum* · Pyrethrum
III *Gaillardia* sp.   IV *Lathyrus grandiflorus* · Everlasting pea

While reproduction
Victorian garden seats are now obtainable, few are likely to match the ornate pattern of this mid-century design. Originals were in cast iron and were extremely heavy. Many modern reproductions are manufactured from light-weight aluminium.

used for this purpose, has no modern counter-part. It matters little whether the lawn is estab-lished with grass or with turf; the basic site preparation is the same although, of course, results are obtained more quickly and more expensively from turf. Two general points must be made. When buying seed, choose a mixture containing rye grass if the lawn is to withstand considerable traffic or general wear and tear. How-ever, this is unlikely to apply to a re-created period garden, and a fine-leaved mixture without rye grass should then be selected. When buying turf, always choose either selected downland turf or specially grown turf. So-called meadow turf is fine for grazing cattle but not for re-creating a Victorian lawn.

ORNAMENTS AND FURNITURE

Perhaps the historical garden features that are most obviously absent from the typical home garden today (or, at least, when present are so conspicu-ously different from the Victorian style) are orna-ments and statuary. All too often, these conjure up images of plastic gnomes and brightly coloured windmills although, fortunately, accurate repro-ductions of garden ornaments representative of many historical periods are increasingly becoming

available. However, it is important to choose care-fully, because an ornament of the wrong period can have a dominating effect, and while many Victorian gardens would, of course, have contained orna-ments dating from earlier times, a contemporary pattern has much to commend it. Urns in stone, reconstituted stone, terra cotta or cast iron were popular, and ornaments in a formal Italian style were especially sought after in the second half of the nineteenth century. Lead has been used since Roman times for water containers, but whereas a nineteenth-century original (or even a replica) cistern with an embossed date would make an admirable feature for a courtyard garden, the price today is likely to be almost prohibitive. Lead was also used sometimes in wellhead pumps, which were made of lead and cast iron, often encased in a

Stone benches *have largely passed from fashion for reasons of cost and weight, but in the right setting they can look magnificent.*

wooden box. These still exist in many British gardens dating from the Victorian period. If your garden already has a well, an original pump for it is certainly worth seeking, especially if it is possible to find one in working order. A modern cast-iron well pump in nineteenth-century style is an acceptable alternative. For a larger well, a purpose-built stone and iron wellhead would be appropriate; many Italian examples were imported into Britain in the nineteenth century although they are difficult to obtain, other than *in situ*, today. Needless to say, the fairy-story wellheads with painted buckets whose inspiration derives principally from Walt Disney are as out of place in the centre of a lawn or a flower bed (where they are normally found) as they would be over a real well.

The choice of statuary is a very personal matter and much hideous material was produced during the nineteenth century (as, of course, it is today). There is no merit, therefore, in buying a piece of appropriate age if you are unable to live with it. Perhaps more than is true of any other item of garden structure, choosing a statue is almost too personal a matter on which to give guidance. It is indeed as difficult as choosing a marriage partner on someone else's behalf. Finally, however, I must mention briefly one or two items that have become popular in some modern gardens and which, although attractive and apparently timeless, were scarcely to be found in Victorian times. The bird bath is essentially a twentieth-century creation that has accompanied our generally increasing concern for wildlife. The Victorians were not so concerned with such things and their birds did their bathing elsewhere. The sundial dates from an earlier age, when people actually used them to tell the time. During the nineteenth century, things mechanical were *de rigueur*, the fob-watch reigned supreme and the sundial faded from appeal. The staddle stone is a seemingly indispensable but functionally useless object in many a British rural garden today. Both originals and replicas are available at very high price, but in the nineteenth century they performed their centuries-old function of supporting grain stores clear of the ground and away from rats.

Furniture is an important garden feature, in an aesthetic as well as a functional sense, and represents one aspect of period gardening for which accurate reproductions are readily available. Examples of the many different styles of Victorian garden chair and table are now produced, either in wood, steel or in cast iron. It is difficult to select the most appropriate from the numerous designs available, but perhaps a short list would include a cast-iron bench, characteristically manufactured in simulated rustic style with ivy-leaf or floral patterning, a cast-iron 'park bench' with slatted wooden seats, a cast-iron or metal and wood tripod table and one (or better still, two) Victorian deck or steamer chairs.

I have left until last perhaps the grandest of the features that you might wish to consider – a garden building. If the garden and the budget are large enough, and the house of appropriate style, a conservatory is well worth considering. There are companies which specialize in custom-built, period-style conservatories but do choose very carefully before parting with large sums of money; I have known a skilled local joiner, builder and glazier to combine forces and produce something at least as good, using traditional skills, at little over half the price. If a conservatory is impossible or inappropriate (and a Gothic folly too ambitious), a summerhouse or one of the typically Victorian wirework arbours now available in reproduction could make a compelling focal point.

Summerhouses are an indulgence and although many patterns are still produced, I doubt if many could compare with this one – yet another instance of the importance of Oriental influences in Victorian gardens.

Conservatories in the Victorian style are very much back in fashion, even in modern gardens. They can be bought as sectional structures or built from scratch on site, the latter quite often a cheaper option.

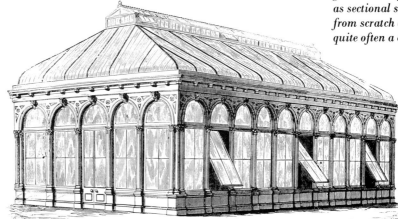

CHAPTER V

BEDDING PLANTS

The half-hardy *zonal pelargonium was one of South Africa's many important contributions to Victorian formal bedding.*

An elaborate carpet *bedding plan, from 'The Gardener's Assistant' by Robert Thompson, published in 1888.*

THE NOTION OF putting plants into a bed still strikes non-gardeners as a rather humorous notion, although the flower bed concept is, in fact, very old. An area called a bed, demarcated from the rest of the garden and used for ornamental plants was first used in the Middle Ages. By the early part of the nineteenth century, the planting and replanting of flower beds through a season, in order to obtain continuity of colour and attractiveness, had become known as bedding or bedding out.

It differed from the planting of borders in several respects. First, in one interpretation at least (exemplified by William Cobbett's definition that I referred to on page 22) a border contained a mixture of many different types of flower, whereas a bed contained many fewer, and very commonly only one type. The bed as a structural entity was also generally several-sided, as opposed to the border which usually had some physical backdrop in the form of a wall or hedge. Moreover, while there are many different types of plant in a typical border, they are not arranged in hard and restricted groupings; indeed, it is a feature of a good border, as I shall be discussing in the next Chapter, that one type, colour and size of plant grades gradually into another. In a flower bed, discretion in planting is the better part of success. But most significantly, whereas the Victorian border was a collection of perennial (and in most cases, hardy perennial) plants, the bed was not. It always was, and still is, essentially an annual feature.

Annual flowers, of course, had been grown in gardens for many hundreds of years before the Victorian period, and a visit to one of the replica Tudor or medieval gardens in Britain now open to the public will reveal collections of marigolds, pansies, and other plants that are familiar today. In these early gardens, however, the plants were largely intermingled, and by my definition were annual borders rather than beds. (Formality in planting certainly was very important in gardens at that time, as I described in Chapter II, but it was generally formality of the permanent planting elements – the box edgings and the shaped shrubs, for instance, rather than of the flowers). Moreover and most importantly, virtually all of the annual plants that comprised these annual borders can be found in a Flora of the wild plants of Britain, or at least of Europe. By definition, they were native and they were hardy.

PROTECTION UNDER GLASS

Two major trends presaged the very different nineteenth-century pattern of bedding. The first was the explosion in global exploration by plant hunters and collectors who sent back seeds gathered on their travels. Sometimes these were gatherings of wild species, native to the areas that they visited. Some-

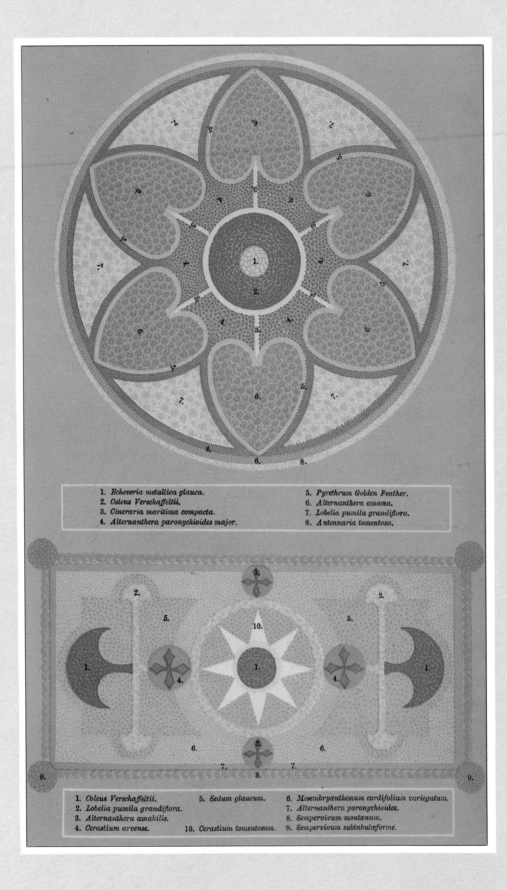

1. *Echeveria metallica glauca.*
2. *Coleus Verschaffeltii.*
3. *Cineraria maritima compacta.*
4. *Alternanthera paronychioides major.*
5. *Pyrethrum Golden Feather.*
6. *Alternanthera amœna.*
7. *Lobelia pumila grandiflora.*
8. *Antennaria tomentosa.*

1. *Coleus Verschaffeltii.*
2. *Lobelia pumila grandiflora.*
3. *Alternanthera amabilis.*
4. *Cerastium arvense.*
5. *Sedum glaucum.*
10. *Cerastium tomentosum.*
6. *Mesembryanthemum cordifolium variegatum.*
7. *Alternanthera paronychioides.*
8. *Sempervivum montanum.*
9. *Sempervivum subtabulæforme.*

times, however, the plant collectors obtained seeds of plants that had been grown over a long period in gardens in these regions and that may well have been subjected to accidental hybridization and deliberate selection for certain desirable features. Whatever their genetic constitution, these newcomers from warmer climes were not able to withstand the adventure of a British winter. But unlike those plants so tender as to be able to survive only with the protection of a building supplied with artificial heating for much of the year (so-called stove plants), many of the new introductions were quite tough enough to perform well outdoors in summer, given a protected start. These plants were called half-hardy annuals, although to be strictly correct, many are in fact perennial in their native climates. The second significant trend that enabled them to have their protected start was the improvement in greenhouse construction that took place throughout the eighteenth century. Greenhouse development was so important for the expansion of bedding in the nineteenth century, that its story bears telling in a little more detail.

Plants require light in order to grow. Hence any building that protects them from the extremes of winter cold must also admit light; and other than on a very small scale (using sheets of mica, for instance), the only material that offered this facility until very recent times was glass. It seems likely that the Romans grew plants in buildings behind protective sheets of glass but obviously the real benefits would only accrue in regions with winters harder than those of the Mediterranean. And it was

not really until the late sixteenth century that structures recognizable as greenhouses ('buildings for overwintering greens') appeared in northern Europe. The 'greens' that were offered protection were usually tender shrubs such as oranges, oleanders and some cypresses.

These early buildings were in fact what we would call orangeries today, for they had solid roofs and glazed walls. They were large, they were expensive and they were very much the preserves of the wealthy who used them as adjuncts to their stately homes. Gradually, smaller versions were built and one-sided structures with glazed roofs appeared. Eventually, the span pattern of greenhouse, glazed all round and in a wide range of sizes, became accepted. But one factor that mitigated against every garden having a greenhouse was the price of glass, which was first taxed in Britain in 1695 and increasingly so from the mid-eighteenth century onwards. Eventually, the cost of sheet glass became so enormous that the entire glass manufacturing industry was threatened. Parliament was persuaded to reduce the burden from about 1820, until the glass tax was finally repealed in 1845 – just in time therefore to capitalize on the potential of the recently introduced tender new plants.

DISPLAY THROUGH THE YEAR

The principle of using the tender bedding plant is to raise the stock initially (and usually with a start in January or February) either from cuttings or from seeds in the warmth of a greenhouse. As the young plants grow, they are pricked on, either into seed boxes (flats) or, in some cases, into individual pots and then, from about April onwards, transferred to cold frames for hardening off. Once the danger of frost has passed, they are planted into prepared beds. Although plants with very short flowering seasons are sometimes removed and replaced with others during the course of the summer, the general trend since the end of the nineteenth century has been that still seen in many parks. In the early part of the year, the beds are occupied with winter-hardy annuals such as winter-flowering pansies, with low growing hardy

An example of 'tessellated colouring' *in beds, published by Hibberd in 1871. The numbers represent individual types of plants and the pattern is repeated in the top half of the plan.*

'Outside Row: *1, 1. Lobelia speciosa; 2. Golden Chain Geranium, dwarf bushy plants. Second Row: 3. Geranium Miss Kingsbury, with flowers picked off; 4, 4. Geranium Little David.* Third Row: *5. Calceolaria aurea floribunda; 6, 6. Dark-leaved Beet.* Centre Row: *7. Centaurea ragusina; 8, 8. Pink Geranium (seedling).*'

Scale: 1cm = 50cm (1in = 4ft).

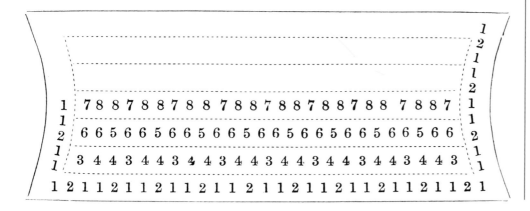

perennials such as primulas that can be lifted, divided and planted elsewhere for growing on during the summer, or with biennials (wallflowers particularly). Often these are interplanted with groups of hardy bulbs, especially with tulips which are amenable to being lifted after flowering in the spring when they are usually heeled into a spare area until the foliage dies down some months later. (Daffodils and most other bulbs resent the disturbance brought about by such lifting until well after they have flowered, and are therefore less amenable to bedding out.) Once the beds are cleared of the winter hardy plants, it is time to bring out the half-hardy subjects which give colourful displays until the first frosts of the autumn kill them off. They in turn are replaced by fresh primulas, pansies, wall-flowers and tulips.

When operating such a scheme, the main cultural considerations to bear in mind relate to feeding, watering and pest and disease problems. After each sequence of plants is lifted, the beds must be refurbished with a fairly slow-release fertilizer to replenish the soil. During the summer growth, regular feeding with a fast-acting liquid fertilizer is essential to promote the continued production of new blooms, while attention to watering is important for these predominantly shallow-rooted yet well-foliaged plants. Pests and diseases can give rise to difficulties in such intensive cultivation where the same small range of plants is being grown continually on the same area of land. The use of healthy seedlings, raised in a sterilized medium, does go a considerable way towards minimizing the introduction of new problems into otherwise uncontaminated soil.

VICTORIAN BEDDING SCHEMES

It is now important to look more closely at the main types of bedding plant, at their relative importance during the different periods of the nineteenth century and to see how they were used to create the characteristic features of the beds of the time.

In the case of plants for the early part of the year, I would add to the list mentioned above the following, less used today in a bedding function than they

would have been one hundred years ago: crocuses, scillas, hyacinths and snowdrops among the bulbs and corms, with alyssum, iberis, forget-me-not (now all but outlawed by mildew), pyrethrums and *Bellis* daisies. Among the half-hardy bedding plants most grown today are ageratums, begonias, *Impatiens* (busy lizzies), lobelias, pelargoniums, petunias and, to a lesser extent, salvias, as well as vast numbers of French, African and Afro-French marigolds and tagetes.

The individual varieties of almost all these half-hardy types are very different from those our grandparents knew, while a few species have also either risen or declined totally in popularity and importance. The various marigolds that I have mentioned were relative latecomers to bedding. The old varieties were extremely pale shadows of the modern forms (what an impact the modern F_1 hybrids would have made in the 1840s), are now quite unobtainable in anything like their original form, and tended to be grown during the mid-nineteenth century only as substitutes for other species. They are really best thought of as twentieth-century plants. Among others, gazanias and tuberous begonias, together with bedding alyssum (actually a hardy plant), came to prominence in the final quarter of the nineteenth century, while verbenas and calceolarias came and went, being significant around the middle of the century but declining and never really regaining much popularity since. (For which, I personally give great thanks, finding that the bedding *Calceolaria* shares with the coxcomb *Celosia* the attribute of

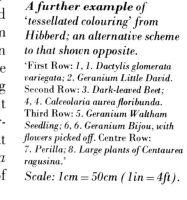

A further example of 'tessellated colouring' from Hibberd; an alternative scheme to that shown opposite.

'First Row: *1, 1. Dactylis glomerata variegata; 2. Geranium Little David.* Second Row: *3. Dark-leaved Beet; 4, 4. Calceolaria aurea floribunda.* Third Row: *5. Geranium Waltham Seedling; 6, 6. Geranium Bijou, with flowers picked off.* Centre Row: *7. Perilla; 8. Large plants of Centaurea ragusina.*'

Scale: 1cm = 50cm (1in = 4ft).

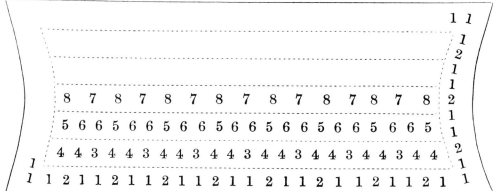

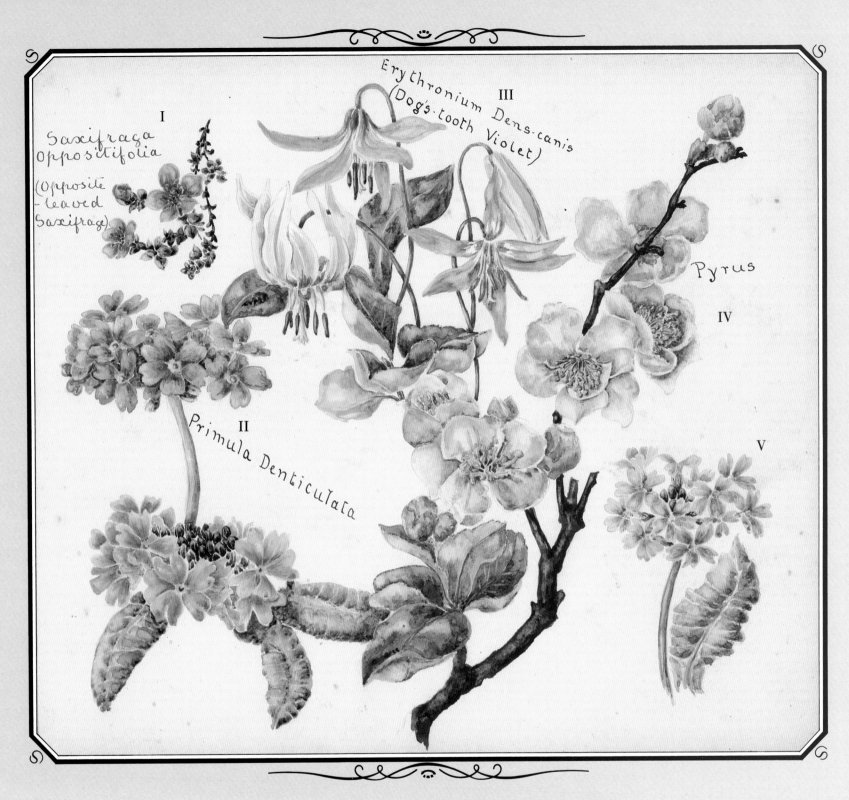

I *Saxifraga oppositifolia*
(Opposite-leaved Saxifrage)

III *Erythronium Dens-canis*
(Dog's-tooth Violet)

Pyrus

II *Primula Denticulata*

I *Saxifraga oppositifolia*   II *Primula denticulata* · Drumstick primula
III *Erythronium dens-canis* · Dog's tooth violet   IV *Pyrus* sp. · Pear
V *Primula denticulata* · Drumstick primula

Ribes Albidum
(White flowering currant)

Dentaria
Pentiphylla
(Five-leaved Toothwort)

Viola biflora
(Yellow Violet)

I *Berberis* sp. (probably *B. angulosa*) **II** *Ribes* sp. · Flowering currant
III *Dentaria pentiphylla* · Five-leaved toothwort **IV** *Viola* sp. · Violet
V *Hyacinthus* · Hyacinth **VI** *Francoa sonchifolia* · Bridal wreath

I *Delphinium* sp.   **II** *Fuchsia* sp.
III *Lysimachia punctata* · Yellow loosestrife

being quite the ugliest flower ever to have been grown in an English garden.) And, to complete the picture, although antirrhinums, bedding dahlias, lantanas and heliotropiums all made their major impact after the end of the nineteenth century, they certainly were grown earlier and can quite safely be included in a late Victorian-style garden today.

All of these, of course, are plants grown especially for their flowers. Most have strong if not strident colours, and they were combined in an almost limitless range of patterns and shapes of bed. Almost every gardening book of the second half of the nineteenth century contains numerous examples of bed patterns and it is with great difficulty that I have selected those included here. I have chosen designs that could be scaled down for a fairly small garden and that include plants not too difficult to obtain today. And although I must stress again that most of the authentically Victorian varieties have vanished, I have given, wherever possible, some hints in the Directory of Plants of which modern types could stand in their stead.

Quite commonly, among the flowering plants of the ornamental beds, the Victorians placed what a garden designer today would call dot plants – individual specimens that form a focal point. Sometimes decidedly tender subtropical species were used for this purpose. Grown in pots, they were taken back under cover and warmth in the autumn. Cannas are those most readily obtained today, but perhaps easier and certainly less expensive are some of the exotic (and exotic looking) but hardier species. Yuccas are excellent, if slow growing, while the taller *Acanthus* looks good and lush.

Apart from these specimen features, all of the bedding plants to which I have referred so far are grown for their flowers. Although the beds in which they were planted and the patterns in which they were arranged were almost invariably more complex than any modern scheme employing the same species, the effect of such a re-creation can be reasonably authentic. However, it was in the massed use of foliage plants that Victorian bedding displayed its most characteristic yet uniquely

curious features, and a re-creation of a small area of Victorian carpet bedding never fails to turn heads and provoke discussion, not least because many of the plants it employs have fallen so much from favour as to have become unfamiliar. Carpet bedding acquired its popular name because the patterns in which the beds were planted simulated the designs on the Oriental carpets, so popular at the time. I mentioned on page 23 some of the foliage plants most important in carpet-bedding designs and more are given in the Directory in Chapter IX. Among the more unlikely, yet effective plants are some of the ornamental versions of vegetables; dwarf beetroots (beets), for instance, were used extensively. Although decidedly unfamiliar to most modern gardeners, seed of many of these foliage plants is not as difficult to obtain as might be imagined, and plants should be raised using the conventional half-hardy technique either from seed or from cuttings. Many of the species require to be stopped or pinched back at least once and sometimes several times in order to stop them from running to flower and also to encourage the compact habit so necessary for optimum effectiveness.

A classic late nineteenth-century design by Hibberd of formal bedding surrounded with gravel and grass. The plants are best listed in the author's own words and here is his suggested planting for 'a harmony in red':

'No. 1, Stella geranium, or an equally rich and heavy crimson scarlet geranium; 2, 2, Blue Lobelia, and a golden-leafed geranium, such as Golden Banner; 3, 3, a dwarf scarlet geranium, such as Attraction or Thomas Moore; 4,4,4,4, same as centre; 5,5,5,5, solid planting of a good rose-pink geranium, like Christine, or Feast of Roses. Nos. 4 and 5 being in the same boundary, and, in fact, one and the same bed, the scarlet must occupy the half nearest the centre, and the pink the other half; 6,6,6,6, Amaranthus melancholicus, edged with Centaurea ragusina; 7, 7, Coleus Verschaffelti, with outer band of yellow Calceolaria; 8, 8, same as 3, 3, and edged with blue Lobelia; 9, 9, a pale pink geranium, such as Pink Muslin, or Rose Queen; 10, 10, Geranium Avalanche, which has white leaves and white flowers.'*

Hibberd gave an alternative planting for 'a harmony in blue':

'No. 1, Petunia Purple Bedder, or Spitfire, or Verbena Celestial Blue, edged with Cerastium; 2, 2, Dwarf Scarlet geranium, edged with blue Lobelia; 3, 3, a tricolor geranium, such as Sunset, or Louisa Smith, edged with blue Lobelia; 4 and 5, in centre of each division of these compartments, about where the figures are placed, a circular dot of a brilliant scarlet geranium, such as Thomas Moore, or Lion Heart, the rest of the block filled in with blue Lobelia, finished with edging of Cerastium; 6,6,6,6, Geranium Flower of Spring, and blue Lobelia, plant and plant, edged with Ivy-leaved Geranium Elegant; 7, 7, a dwarf scarlet geranium, edged with blue Lobelia; 8, 8, Lobelia Indigo Blue, edged with Geranium Flower of Spring; 9, 9, a lilac or rose-pink geranium, such as Lilac Banner, Feast of Roses, or Amy Hogg; 10,10, a dwarf salmon or orange-scarlet geranium, such as H.W. Longfellow, or Harkaway, edged with Cerastium.'*

Scale: 1cm = 3m (2in = 50ft).

CHAPTER VI

THE HERBACEOUS BORDER

ALMOST ANYONE having more than a passing acquaintance with gardening could be expected to name the herbaceous border as the garden feature conjured up more than any other by thoughts of the Victorian age. Such a border must therefore be an integral part of any modern reconstruction of a late nineteenth-century garden. In fact, as I mentioned in Chapter II, the name of one nineteenth-century gardener, Gertrude Jekyll, has become so closely associated in many people's minds with this aspect of gardening that herbaceous borders are sometimes referred to as 'Jekyll' borders or as

Gertrude Jekyll (1843-1932) was one of the great figures of nineteenth-century gardening. She discovered the value of the herbaceous border and made it the central feature of the numerous gardens that she designed. Her most celebrated work was that done in collaboration with the architect Edwin Lutyens.

borders of the Jekyll type. Because of this popular over-generalization, because of a widespread misconception that the splendid Miss Jekyll actually invented the herbaceous border, and because there is still considerable misunderstanding over exactly what constituted a herbaceous border in the Victorian sense, a little background information is appropriate before I consider the details of planning and planting.

First, a definition of the adjective 'herbaceous'. To the botanist, a herbaceous plant (or, as it is called for short, a herb – in the broad, not the culinary, sense) is simply a plant that is not dependent for its physical support upon wood. Some of its tissues may be toughened to help it remain upright, but when winter comes, the above-ground parts die down. Thus a herbaceous plant differs significantly from a tree or shrub, which remains permanently above ground in a more or less dormant or resting state (either with its leaves, in the case of evergreens, or without, in the case of deciduous types).

Herbaceous plants can be subdivided further into the two main categories of annuals (which figured largely in Chapter V) and perennials. When annuals die down at the end of the season, the plant expires totally, and survival of the species to the next season is solely through the medium of seeds. By contrast, the herbaceous perennial survives as a plant but, unlike the tree or shrub, it

A Summer Herbaceous Border by Lillian Stannard.

Phlox

I

III

Echinops
ruthenicus
(Globe Thistle.)

Hemerocallis
fulva fl. pl. II

(Double
Day Lily)

I *Phlox* sp. · Phlox   II *Hemerocallis* sp. · Day lily   III *Echinops ritro*

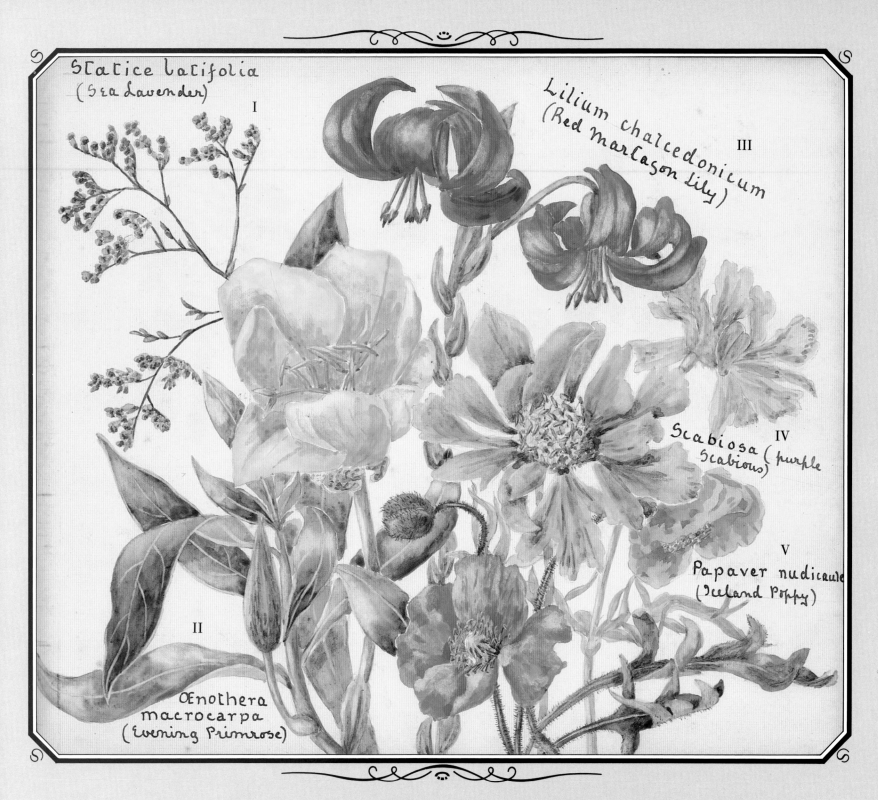

Statice latifolia
(Sea Lavender)
I

Lilium chalcedonicum
(Red Martagon Lily)
III

Scabiosa (purple
Scabious)
IV

Papaver nudicaule
(Iceland Poppy)
V

II

Œnothera
macrocarpa
(Evening Primrose)

I *Limonium latifolium (= Statice latifolia)* · Statice
II *Oenothera missouriensis* · Evening primrose   III *Lilium chalcedonicum*
IV *Scabiosa* sp. · Purple scabious   V *Papaver nudicaule* · Iceland poppy

Lutyens, and began a partnership that was to have a truly enduring effect on the English garden scene. As Lutyens designed houses, so Jekyll took care of their gardens and planted them with vision. Although fairly considered Victorian, it should not be forgotten that the Jekyll-Lutyens partnership lasted well into our own century; Hestercombe House in Somerset, dating from 1906, is for me the apogee of their collaboration.

I do feel that Gertrude Jekyll had so much to show us about garden design in general that even a very brief dip into her writings is instructive. Perhaps the greatest of Jekyll's teachings lies in her use of colour. She was a frustrated painter and embroiderer (frustrated through poor eyesight), and this shows in her garden plans. Herbaceous borders can be attractive, sometimes very attractive, even when they are what is known popularly as 'riots of colour'. In such a massed planting, with a wide range of plant shapes, you can actually get away with a hotchpotch of reds, yellows and blues, provided there is some sense in the plant heights: the tallest at the back and the shortest at the front. But not many of Jekyll's borders were riots of colour. They were more clever and more subtle; and, at the end of the day, I believe more majestic too. One of their most characteristic colour features lay in their use of cool colours towards the sides, with hotter and more fiery shades in the centre. In fact, the use of cool colours in general – whites, silvers and, of course, green – was very much a Gertrude Jekyll hallmark, and I have long felt that there is much to be said for considering green and white the most important colours in a garden.

Verbascum olympicum. *The verbascums or mulleins were much loved by Gertrude Jekyll and provide tall, stately features for the back of the herbaceous border although unfortunately few species are truly perennial.*

For optimum effect, *a herbaceous border should be backed against some vertical structure, preferably a wall, as here at Sidbury Manor.*

PROVIDING CONTINUITY OF COLOUR

Another important Jekyll message (too readily forgotten today, but an important consideration for anyone re-creating a period border) is that to maintain continuity of colour right through the summer is impossible; doubly so with the restrictions on overall size imposed by modern gardens. You have two choices: either to have several small herbaceous borders, restricting the flowering time of each to a period of a few weeks; or to have one large border and maintain a substantial stock of plants in pots for moving into and out again as their flowering seasons arise.

Given these two possible approaches, therefore, I must first suggest to you the two Jekyll summer borders shown in the plans on pages 66-7, one for light and one for heavy soils. Miss Jekyll intended these to be 24 m (78 ft) long but the sizes of the individual plant groups could be scaled down to modern proportions. And in some instances, of course, the available plants nearest to her sometimes scant descriptions must be used – the bald 'Delphinium', for example, gives you plenty of scope.

A second alternative is to take a Jekyll scheme for a July to September border which could either be copied more or less in its entirety or if space is limited, any of the three individual monthly components could be planted up as separate borders. And I can bring the whole to life no better than by describing it in the lady's own words: 'One end in July – to name some of the more important flowers – would have Delphinium, white lily, white foxglove and Eryngium, with foamy masses of the bushy Clematis recta and white tree lupin, passing to the pale yellow of Thalictrum, mullein, the tall Oenothera and the pale yellow day lily; then onwards in strength of colour in Alstroemeria, orange day lily and the fine Lilium croceum, to the scarlet of Lychnis chalcedonica. The sequence of colour would then again proceed by orange and yellow to the far end, where there would be Galega white and purple, Chrysanthemum maximum, the tall white campanulas, macrantha and persicifolia and white everlasting pea, with the splendid

Lilium sp.

Lupinus Lepida
(Lupine)
I

Lupinus
polyphylius
II

Lindelophia
spectabilis
(Boragewort)
III

Hemerocallis
Day Lily
IV

I *Lupinus lepidus* · Lupin   **II** *Lupinus polyphyllus* · Lupin
III *Lindelofia longiflora*   **IV** *Hemerocallis* sp. · Day lily

I *Lilium pyrenaicum*   **II** *Dictamnus fraxinella* · Burning bush

Gertrude Jekyll's suggested arrangement for a border of perennials on light soil (plants as named by Jekyll).

purple of Campanula macrocarpa and the noble crane's bill, Geranium ibericum. These will be followed in August by Anemone japonica, white and pink; Echinops, Erigeron, Gypsophila, Lilium longiflorum at the cool ends, and hollyhock, Helenium, Penstemon, red Phlox etc in the middle. September would bring in a further succession of the blaze of Dahlia, Gladiolus, Tritoma, Helianthus and Canna for the middle glory, and Clematis flammula, white Dahlia, Hydrangea and the earlier Michaelmas daisies at the cool-coloured ends.'

is a craft to be learned by degrees. Anyone who has grown delphiniums (and there can't be many gardeners who haven't) will know that once flowering is over by late summer, the dead seed heads are not the most beautiful objects in the border and are best cut away. But anyone who has grown the delightful small white-flowered *Clematis flammula* (and there can't be many gardeners who have) will know that it needs support to show off its early autumn blossom to the full. Plant it with the delphiniums, said Jekyll, cut away the top part of their old flowering shoots, leaving 1.2 m (4 ft)

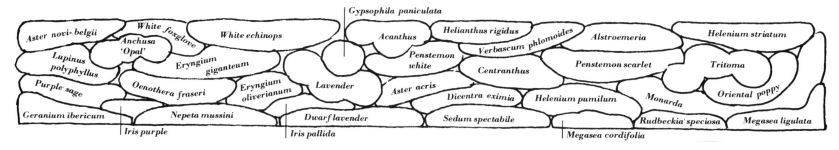

Miss Jekyll went on to say that these were the most important hardy plants (and interestingly enough, she considered *Canna* and *Dahlia* among them) and that the best of the half-hardy annuals should be used also – dwarf tropaeolums, African marigolds, annual sunflowers, stocks, China asters and snapdragons were suggested. Nor did she exclude the best of 'the so-called bedding plants' – pelargoniums, calceolarias, salvias, gazanias and heliotropes – from taking their place in and near the front. Great importance was attached also to 'between' plants such as rosemary, lavender, *Phlomis*, ornamental grasses, lavender cotton, *Stachys* and pinks to set off the more showy flowers; and some of these could also be grown in pots and brought into the border to fill gaps or help colour contrasts. Pots of *Lilium longiflorum, Lilium auratum, Campanula pyramidalis* and hydrangeas were thought especially useful, too, in this infilling role.

One example of Jekyll's ideas displays to me most clearly not only her colour sense but her gardening skill too. It indicates also that the creation of a successful Victorian-style herbaceous border

standing, and thus give the clematis a framework to show off itself. So simple, isn't it, when you have been shown? 'By watching a flower border carefully,' the lady said, 'and noting the ways and wants of its occupants one may invent and practise many such devices, both to the benefit of its appearance and also much to one's own interest and amusement.'

THE PRACTICAL CONSIDERATIONS

And so to some of the more basic aspects of recreating the Victorian border. First, the problem of obtaining specific plants, which it must be admitted is not fully surmountable. When Jekyll and her contemporaries spoke of border flowers, they rather seldom referred to them by varietal name. In many instances, this was because the only forms available were the more or less wild species – in fact, Victorian gardening books often spoke of named varieties as *garden* varieties, implying that they were somewhat out of the ordinary in existing as such. In other instances, named varieties certainly did exist and in a proportion of cases these may still be obtained today, for some cultivated varieties of herbaceous perennials have survived unchanged from the Victorian period, or even earlier. Examples are given in the Directory of Plants in Chapter IX.

Siting the border should not present too much difficulty, for most gardens have at least one area that receives sun for most of the day. I do not wish to imply that a herbaceous border of sorts cannot be planted in a shady area but it will be (almost literally), a pale shadow of the real thing. The typical Victorian border backed onto a wall although a fence is fine and even a hedge will suffice at a stretch.

preparation was seen as essential to the establishment of a successful border. Carefully clear out perennial weed growth on the chosen area (although with modern herbicides, all is not lost if a little escapes your attention) and incorporate, preferably by double digging, quantities of well-rotted manure or compost. Although individual plants can, indeed should, be lifted and divided every few years, the border as a whole is most unlikely to be disturbed for a long time. The incorporating of organic matter, other than as surface mulch, to improve the soil in an established

A suggested arrangement by Gertrude Jekyll for a border of perennials on heavy soil (plants as named by Jekyll).

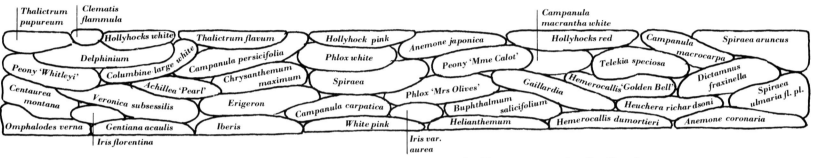

Borders of the time were not typically island borders, however, and groups of herbaceous perennials grown in a sea of lawn are really hallmarks of twentieth- rather than nineteenth-century gardening. Given some form of backing to provide visual as much as physical support, a herbaceous border can be of almost any length and almost any depth. Nevertheless, a border less than about 2 m (6 ft) deep and 5-8 m (16-25 ft) long will almost certainly fail if it is intended to provide real continuity of colour and interest for more than about six weeks. Unless you are prepared to go to the great additional trouble of moving potted plants in and out of the border.

Miss Jekyll herself did not usually indicate the actual numbers of individual plants needed, but some good modern catalogues suggest the numbers of plants of each type needed to plant up 1 sq. m (10 sq. ft), and calculations of totals required can thus be made accordingly. And although I have suggested sample plans, do be inventive. Again, a good catalogue will help you in supplying details of flowering times and heights.

In the nineteenth century, as now, good site

border is no easy task. Even so, regular feeding is vitally important, and top dressing with a modern balanced fertilizer as growth begins in the spring, followed by regular application of liquid fertilizers during the growing season, should be a routine. Surface mulch should also be applied in spring to maintain the soil in moist, cool condition, although the importance of additional watering during the summer must not be minimized. Modern technology can help here. A perforated sprinkler hosepipe laid through the border at the start of the season will soon be obscured by the growing plants, and so can be connected to a mains supply as needed to provide gentle but unobtrusive irrigation.

Finally, a note on the all-important subject of staking. Almost no herbaceous perennials will appear at their best without some form of artificial support – the more so with old, less robust varieties. Far and away the best and most appropriate support is provided by twigs, pushed unobtrusively around each clump. Small canes with raffia or jute are acceptable too, but modern wire or interlocking metallic supports are inappropriate.

CHAPTER VII

ROSES IN THE VICTORIAN GARDEN

THE ROSE is understandably regarded by many people as the garden flower *par excellence*. But to talk of *the* rose as if it was but a single variety or even a single species is misleading to an alarming degree; more misleading, indeed, than in the case of any other garden flower, fruit, tree or vegetable.

Rose growing in Britain first began to attain its present dizzy heights of popularity in the latter half of the nineteenth century. The first national rose show had been held in 1858 and the National Rose Society was formed in 1876. Books on the subject of rose growing began to appear in ever increasing numbers and none was more popular than the eminently simply titled *A Book About Roses* by The Reverend S. Reynolds Hole, Dean of Rochester, first published in 1869, which ran to numerous editions, many of them still readily obtainable. Hole had been responsible for that first national show and, under the subject of Garden Roses, discussed in his book the merits of a dozen or more major different groups of rose; an astonishing range for the modern gardener accustomed to think of roses as either Large-flowered (Hybrid Teas) or Cluster-flowered (Floribundas). How did so many types of rose come to exist and why was it that the late Victorian gardener clearly had his favourites, while hedging his bets?

The origins of rose cultivation are lost in the mists of antiquity but undoubtedly some of those that graced the Victorian garden had been gracing other gardens for a very long time. For hundreds of years, before mere men had learned the art of deliberate plant hybridization, the roses grown in cultivation were of two main types. They were selections of plants either from among natural species growing wild in various parts of the world or from natural hybrids, having arisen at some undetermined date through the pollinating activities of a wandering bee. By the late eighteenth century, however, artificial hybridization had become possible and relatively few of the really ancient roses of natural origin were still grown. Even so, it was possible to recognize characteristics in the old varieties that suggested something of their parentage and ancestry; hence new and artificially raised varieties would often be classified with them. The most important groupings among the ancient roses were the Centifolias and Moss roses, Damasks, Gallicas, Portlands, Albas, Chinas and, of course, the species.

DISTANT ORIGINS

The Provence or Centifolia roses ('roses of a hundred petals') may have a truly ancient origin because many-petalled roses had been described in antiquity. Varieties were certainly proliferating dramatically by the fifteenth and sixteenth centuries and were recorded for posterity on the can-

The moss roses with their masses of soft, almost moss-like prickles date from the late seventeenth century and have a particularly evocative appeal.

Crimson Rambler at Clandon Park, *Surrey, by Thomas Hunn.*

Rosa centifolia, *the Provence or Cabbage rose, is a representative of a very ancient group of richly perfumed, many-petalled roses.*

vases of many contemporary artists. They are now known to have an extremely complex ancestry – so complex that it is hard to believe that they arose without human intervention. Their flowers resemble voluptuous females, big, blowsy and beautiful, painted, perfumed and nonchalant. The plants are big, too, given to sprawling yet splendid, abundantly thorny and with coarse grey-green foliage. They declined in favour during the Victorian period but among those still in cultivation by the 1890s were 'Blanchefleur', 'Bullata', 'De Meaux', 'Petite de Hollande' and 'White' or 'Unique Provence'.

The individual and arguably charming Moss roses bear a mass of moss-like, soft bristles on the stems and especially on and around the buds. They are particularly appealing when the buds burst, although later many are something of a let-down. They seem to have started life with a chance sport from a Centifolia in the late seventeenth century but the Victorian hybridists took them to their hearts, and 'Alfred de Dalmas', 'À Longs Pedoncules', 'Blanche Moreau', 'Common Moss', 'Japonica', 'Salet' and 'White Bath', among two or three dozen more, would find a place in the beds.

Gallica roses are derived from *Rosa gallica*, a true species which is found wild across wide areas of southern Europe and southwestern Asia, and which is an ancestor of many modern roses. The Gallicas tend to be rather low-growing shrubs, ideal for the smaller garden, but with a fairly upright habit, often somewhat sparsely thorned and well scented. Ancient forms still widely cultivated, at least as curiosities, in Victorian times were the 'Red Rose of Lancaster' and its striped sport 'Rosa Mundi' or 'Village Maid', the former variant being supposedly named after Fair Rosamund, mistress of Henry II. Later hybrids of Gallica roses would have found at least a modicum of representatives in most Victorian gardens, and rightly so, as the group includes a few gems: 'Belle de Crécy', 'Duchesse d'Angoulême', 'Hippolyte', 'Nestor', the gloriously deep velvet red 'Tuscany Superb' and perhaps the striped 'Georges Vibert'.

Clearly allied to the Gallica roses, although by what routes is arguable, are the Damasks. And if ever the word perfume was synonymous with roses, then it is surely best associated with the Damasks, for they are possessed of the rich fragrance that more than anything else conjures up images of the rose garden on a balmy evening at the height of summer. They tend to grow taller than Gallicas, with arching stems well furnished with thorns and with flowers in the subtlest shades of pink. Although of ancient origin, the relatively few Damask rose varieties to be found in the nineteenth century would probably have been at most 300 years old, for the type seems to have been all but lost to cultivation for long periods. They are usually divided into the summer-flowering and the so-called autumn-flowering (in fact, repeat-flowering) types, each with somewhat different ancestry. Among the former, the sumptuous white 'Madame Hardy' and the pink flecked 'Leda', both from the early part of the nineteenth century, would have found a welcome home in most Victorian rose gardens, alongside the repeat-blooming and very much older 'Quatre Saisons'.

A rose type that proved both popular and valuable for the Victorian gardener was the Portland, a compact plant, splendid for the small garden and with that immense virtue of a long flowering season. Its origins are disputed but it was probably a cross between a Damask and a Gallica. I say 'it', really in reference to the original crimson eighteenth-century plant called 'The Portland Rose' or 'Duchess of Portland', although by the late Victorian period the range had extended to include others, most notably the double white 'Blanc de Vibert', and the gorgeous rich pink 'Comte de Chambord'.

Just as a Gallica was the Red Rose of Lancaster, so the White Rose of York was an Alba, one of a group of superb roses of uncertain but ancient origin, typically strong-growing, lusty, perfumed and pink, although also with some glorious whites, as their name suggests. They, too, had fallen somewhat from grace for Dean Hole and his contemporaries, although few gardeners of worth would not have found a home for the ancient 'Great Maiden's Blush' (sometimes less modestly called 'Cuisse de Nymphe'), 'Celestial' and their Victorian companion 'Königin von Dänemark'. One of the incidental advantages of the Albas was their general freedom from disease.

FROM EAST AND WEST

China was the source of so much that was good in the late nineteenth-century garden that it would have been surprising indeed if it did not also contribute roses. Although the plant actually known as *Rosa chinensis* seems to have disappeared from the wild (if ever it was a truly wild species), a gradual trickle of Chinese garden hybrids began to reach Britain through India in the early part of the eighteenth century. (*Rosa chinensis*, incidentally, was sometimes called *Rosa indica*, a specific epithet accorded a number of other Oriental plants which were brought to the West through the good services of the East India Company.) Some of these early Chinese garden names persisted, and most late-Victorian rose gardens would include the two best of them, 'Old Blush', also called 'Parson's Pink' or 'Common Monthly' (the latter a reference to its repeat-flowering characteristics) and the deep velvet, low-growing 'Old Crimson'.

Of the rose types that were essentially born of the nineteenth century, it is with *Rosa chinensis* that we must start, and almost finish too, for its importance was huge and far-reaching. Among the hybrids derived more or less directly from the original Chinese hybrids, few were more popular

THE NORTH AMERICAN ROSE EXPERIENCE

Because of the tremendous importance for rose growing and rose breeding of the species introduced to Europe from China, there is sometimes a tendency to forget two things. First that the original cross between a European rose and the new Chinese introductions was actually made by John Champeney of Charleston, South Carolina. And second that there are many rose species native to North America too. The small shrubby *Rosa suffulta* and *R. carolina* and the taller *R. californica*, *R. blanda* and *R. virginiana* and the climbing *R. setigera* are among the best known. They tend to be later flowering than the European species but almost all have splendid autumn colour.

American rose breeding during the nineteenth century lagged far behind that taking place in Europe, although a similar range of varieties was popular; the Osborne Nursery in California, for instance, listed around one hundred imported hybrid perpetual varieties in 1855. America had its personalities too; early in the century the Scots born Robert Buist, whose popular 'Rose Manual' was published in 1844, was instrumental in bringing many choice European hybrids to his adopted land. Later, Henry B. Ellwanger proclaimed the need for American rose breeders to rise to the challenge and produce varieties more suited to the American climate. The American Rose Society just managed to be a nineteenth-century foundation, being established in 1899, and, of course, throughout the twentieth century, American rose raisers have been well able to hold their own.

Rosa californica

Hydrangea paniculata grandiflora
I

Leycesteria formosa
II

III

I *Hydrangea paniculata 'Grandiflora'*　II *Leycesteria formosa*
III *Symphoricarpos* sp. · Snowberry

I *Rosa rugosa*
II *Daboecia cantabrica (= Menziesia polifolia)* · St Dabeoc's heath
III *Styrax japonica*

than the dainty little pink buttonhole rose, 'Cécile Brunner' and the semi-double red 'Cramoisie Supérieur'. Of the entirely new groupings, first must come the Bourbons, a race of roses that began life, most improbably, on the island of Réunion (then called the Ile de Bourbon) in the Indian Ocean, with *Rosa chinensis* as one parent and an Autumn Damask the other. And what a wonderful lineage they were, fragrant, fairly well disciplined in growth, predominantly rich pink in colour and repeat-flowering. Although they had begun to decline in favour as the century drew to a close, the best were still indispensable and no gardener worthy of the name would not have had 'Madame Isaac Péreire', 'Souvenir de la Malmaison', 'La Reine Victoria' (of course!) and, perhaps most valuable of all, the thornless climber 'Zéphirine Drouhin'.

Of greater popularity still were the Noisette roses, raised first in the southern states of America by one John Champney and taken up by his neighbour, Philippe Noisette, using 'Old Blush' as an original parent. They tend to come into bloom rather later than Bourbons but some flower almost continuously thereafter. The original variety, 'Champney's Pink Cluster', and its first seedling 'Blush Noisette', remained popular; but perhaps the greatest appeal of this group lay in its several yellow members such as 'Céline Forestier' and 'Desprez à Fleurs Jaunes', although the most glorious of all Victorian white climbers, 'Mme Alfred Carrière' belongs here as well.

TEAS AND HYBRIDS

The Hybrid Perpetuals, which above all dominated the second half of the nineteenth century, were an extremely diverse assemblage, sharing ancestry only in the Bourbons. They were, as their name indicates, simply roses of hybrid origin and repeat, if not strictly perpetual, flowering. From the thousand or more varieties in existence at the end of the Victorian period, only a few can be chosen, but being those that have survived to the present day, at least they possess the attribute of durability. And the best are extremely beautiful,

although not always easy to cultivate, because their habit is often of an upright plant with its bloom concentrated at the top and somewhat bare below. Given a choice of half a dozen, representing the best that the group and the period could offer, the list might be 'Baron de Bonstetten', 'Baroness Rothschild', 'Crown Prince', 'Dembrowski', 'Dupuy Jamain' and, loveliest of all, 'Reine des Violettes'.

The group of Chinese rose derivatives with the greatest significance of all for the modern gardener (although they only began to assume real importance as the century closed) was that of the Tea-scented roses. These flowers evidently acquired their name from the chests in which tea was transported from the Orient. Apparently they originated in a cross between *Rosa chinensis* and a phenomenal eastern wonder called *Rosa gigantea*. The first variety to arrive in Britain was 'Hume's Blush', a rose of very variable colour and form, from almost yellow to pink and from single to semi-double. The second, in 1824, was 'Park's Yellow Tea-Scented China', a rose that gave the valuable colour to the later Noisettes; but it was this variety and one of Robert Fortune's prizes, 'Fortune's Double Yellow', that were responsible for bringing yellow into prominence in the late-century rose garden as these original Chinese introductions gave rise to the race of roses that soon became known simply as Teas. Despite their reputation, to an extent justified, of being tender, some are of stout constitution (although it is doubtful how well they would have fared at Seggieden). Among the indispensables would be 'Sombreuil', a rose second only to 'Mme Alfred Carrière' as a Victorian white climber (but much less vigorous), 'The Bride', another almost white rose that found its way into royal wedding bouquets of the period, and, of course, the apricot orange 'Gloire de Dijon'.

Sooner or later, someone was bound to cross a Tea rose with a Hybrid Perpetual. This was a Monsieur Guillot, who launched 'La France' in 1867, the first of the race of roses that became known as Hybrid Teas (and more recently as

Gloire de Dijon

'large-flowered bush roses'). Over the succeeding thirty years (and, of course, since), their long flowering season and attractive flower form stimulated a huge following, although it must be said that many of the early varieties were of somewhat weak constitution. In the Victorian garden, worthy companions to the pink 'La France' could be found in the creamy white 'Grace Darling' and the red 'Reine Marie Henriette', one of a small group that heralded a few superb climbing Hybrid Teas in the early years of this century.

THE CLIMBERS

Among some of the smaller groups and species significant for the Victorians was a rose destined to be a parent of many hybrids (largely in the early years after Victoria's death) but always popular as a species. This was the single Japanese *Rosa rugosa*, its rough, most un-rose-like foliage having the immense virtue of almost total freedom from disease. Another was the most famous of all the Orientals – if only because of its reputed (and, to some degree, real) tenderness – the glorious pale yellow climber, *Rosa banksiae lutea*. Brought from China in the 1820s, it has been a challenge to rose growers ever since. A third rose to be found in most Victorian rose catalogues came much earlier, the species now called *Rosa foetida* or 'Austrian Briar'. Originating in Asia and known in Britain since the sixteenth century, it had a special appeal in the days when almost all

roses were shades of pink or red, for its flowers were yellow. Nevertheless, the craving for yellow among rose growers and, indeed, its gradual prominence toward the end of the nineteenth century, brought to the garden a rose disease hitherto scarcely worth a mention – black spot.

A fact often forgotten by modern gardeners is that the choice in climbing roses was extremely restricted in Victorian gardens, and the rambler as we understand it was almost non-existent in gardens before *Rosa wichuraiana* was introduced from China in 1860. 'Alberic Barbier', 'Albertine', 'American Pillar', 'New Dawn' and 'Dr W. Van Fleet', for instance, are all twentieth-

Rosa foetida, *the Austrian briar, grew at Seggieden. It probably originated before the sixteenth century and this form, the 'Austrian Copper', is a particularly vivid coppery orange.*

I *Phlomis samia* · Jerusalem sage II *Deutzia scabra*
III *Rosa foetida (= punicea)* · Austrian briar

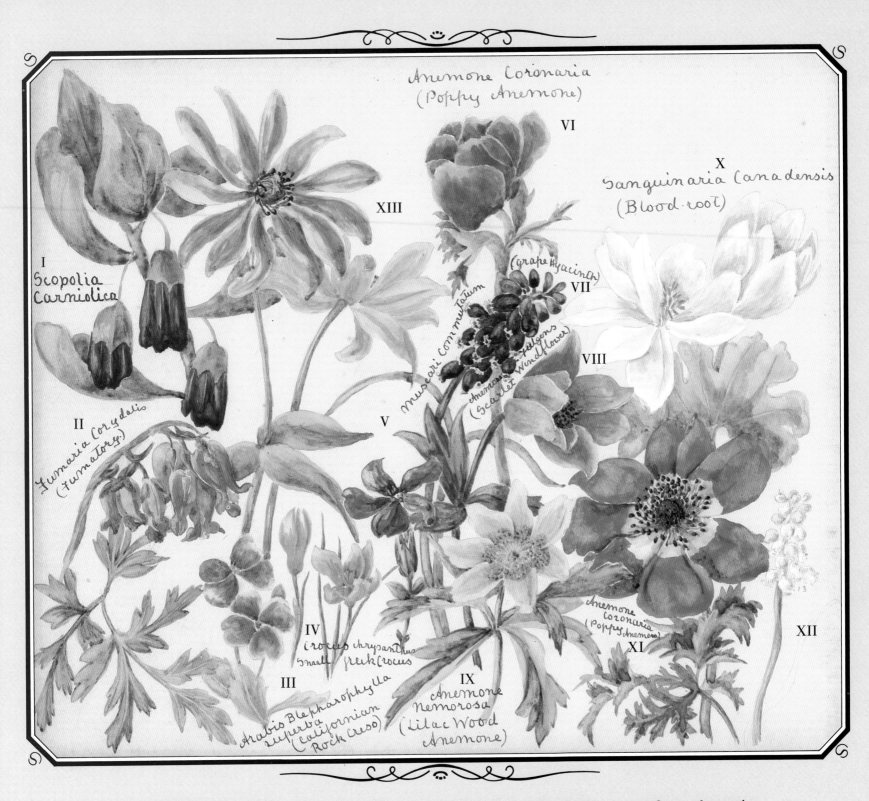

Anemone Coronaria
(Poppy Anemone)

VI

X

Sanguinaria Canadensis
(Blood-root)

XIII

I
Scopolia
Carniolica

(Grape Hyacinth)

VII

Muscari commutatum

Anemone fulgens
(Scarlet Windflower)

VIII

II
Fumaria (Corydalis
Fumatory)

V

XII

Anemone
coronaria
(Poppy anemone)

XI

IV
Crocus chrysanthus
Small freak Crocus

III
Arabis Blepharophylla
superba
(Californian
Rock Cress)

IX
Anemone
Nemorosa
(Lilac Wood
Anemone)

I *Scopolia carniolica*   **II** *Corydalis* sp. · Fumitory   **III** *Arabis blepharophylla* · Rock cress   **IV** *Crocus chrysanthus*

V *Gentiana verna* · Spring gentian   **VI** *Anemone coronaria* · Poppy anemone   **VII** *Muscari commutatum* · Grape hyacinth

VIII *Anemone × fulgens*   **IX** *Anemone nemorosa*   **X** *Sanguinaria canadensis* · Blood root

XI *Anemone coronaria* · Poppy anemone   **XII** *Muscari* sp. · Grape hyacinth   **XIII** *Dimorphotheca* sp.(?)

*A **rose-festooned** cottage from William Robinson's 'The English Flower Garden', first published in 1883, showing how ordered informality is called for. Neatly trained plants on trellis would be out of place here.*

yellowish pink 'Lord Penzance' is the oldest still in existence. And, finally, a mention of the so-called Boursault roses, largely thornless climbers of China origin. The first few of them were raised in the early years of the nineteenth century by a Monsieur Henri Boursault and the group was still listed at the end of the era as 'Very good climbers'. Useful survivors are the crimson-purple 'Amadis' and the lovely pink 'Madame Sancy de Parabère'.

COMPOSITION AND DESIGN

As with most other aspects of flower gardening, there were differences of opinion among Victorian gardeners as to the way that roses should be displayed to best advantage. But more than with most other aspects of flower gardening, the options were large because the plants themselves assumed such varied form. In an attempt to make life reasonably simple, I shall consider only the overall objectives of the two main schools of gardening thought – one being to have a rose garden as a separate entity; and the other, so strongly advocated towards the end of the century, to integrate roses more completely into the remainder of the flower garden. In the former, the rose enthusiast could, within a limited area, take guests on a conducted tour through the genus *Rosa* in all its diversity, could compare and contrast the merits, virtues and vices of the various groups, species and varieties, and use the subtle variations in reds, pinks and whites to create patterns of colour. The garden could be three-dimensional through the careful use of pergolas, arches, trellises and pillars and, of course, plants of different heights, but (and it was, at least until the latter half of the nineteenth century, rather a large 'but') there was no continuity of colour. Until the advent of the bulk of the recurrent-flowering varieties, the rose garden was a garden of early summer. But for some growers, this brevity was, and still is, more than recompensed by the sheer overpowering visual and aromatic impact of the whole. Even within the realm of the dedicated rose garden, there could be a range from the essentially simple to the essentially complex, and from the large to the not so large.

century roses. Hence the reference in gardening books of the Victorian period to types of climbing or scrambling roses that are only grown today, if at all, as curios. Best known perhaps were the Ayrshire roses such as 'Dundee Rambler' and 'Ayrshire Queen', derived from the common field rose, *Rosa arvensis*, but of which sadly few varieties survive. The old 'Sweet Briar', *Rosa eglanteria*, similarly gave rise to numerous scrambling shrubs, of which the best known were those in the group called Lord Penzance's Sweet Briars. Probably the

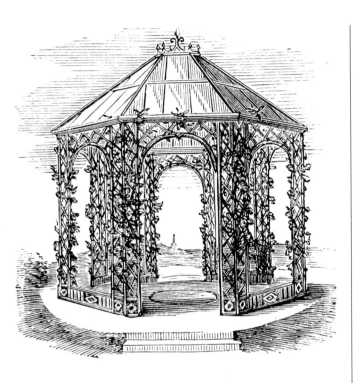

The actual siting of the dedicated rose garden, be it large or small, within the garden as a whole offers two choices: close to the house, like the flower beds of the landscaped gardens of the eighteenth century (when, thanks to the landscaping, there was really nowhere else for them to go); or some distance away. The latter was, and is, to be preferred for two main reasons. First, even the devotee of roses (or as Hibberd put it so colourfully, the man was half-mad on the subject) would have to admit that outside its peak flowering season, the Victorian rose garden was a thing of less than the greatest beauty. Second, a rosary in its full glory was a creation that embodied an element of surprise and mystery, to be sought and discovered beyond a hedge, through an archway or round a corner. It should not be immediately obvious or yield up its treasures without some effort by the beholder.

Other gardeners argued, however, that the reason the rose had to be planted only with other roses and almost out of sight was that it was not a truly decorative plant and achieved its effect solely through force of numbers. But by the time William

Robinson was writing, at the end of the century, the rose in flower was no longer quite the nine-days' wonder it had been, and the Hybrid Perpetuals and especially the Teas and Hybrid Teas were considered fit to be seen in decent company – 'back to the flower garden with them,' he said.

And so the Robinsonian roses were displayed in small groups, often of individual types – half a dozen Tea roses here, a massed planting of Hybrid Perpetuals there, perhaps with yellow climbing Teas on the walls. Sometimes they were interplanted with other perennials (one has only to see 'Tuscany Superb' among a bed of lavender to appreciate the force of the Robinson message). And occasionally they were literally mixed in with the other inhabitants of the herbaceous border in a manner that even today is arguably underdone and misunderstood.

Not all Victorian gardens grew roses in a natural manner. This late nineteenth-century rose temple represents the other extreme of climbing rose cultivation.

ROSE CULTIVATION THEN AND NOW

The subject of William Robinson neatly brings us to the Victorian techniques of cultivation. To be true to *his* ideal, roses would be grown, not in 'raw beds of manure and pruned hard and set thin so as to develop large blooms', but mulched as often as not with a living carpet of pansies, violets and other rock plants, for Robinson considered that covering beds near the house with 'excreta from the farm' was 'neither sanitary nor necessary'. His view was contrary to the general practice of the period which encouraged very heavy dependence on manures, or more specifically, on soil well-dunged with farmyard manure and farmyard manure alone – 'the treasure', as Dean Hole called it. And this remains the generally advocated practice today. There is no more effective preparation for the rose plant than the thorough incorporation into the soil of well-rotted manure or compost in advance of planting. The importance of mulching is now also widely acknowledged, and although the most modern introduction, shredded bark, would have no place in an authentically reconstructed Victorian garden, it is undeniably more acceptable socially than 'excreta from the farm', as Robinson put it.

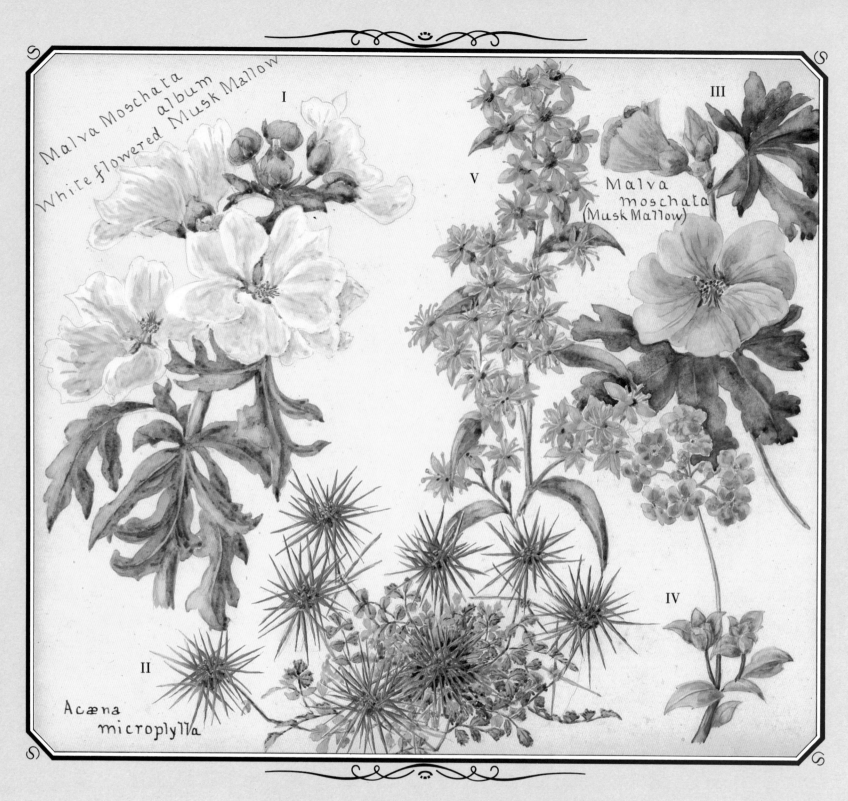

Malva Moschata album
White flowered Musk Mallow

I

III

V

Malva
moschata
(Musk Mallow)

II

Acæna
microplylla

IV

I *Malva moschata* · Musk mallow   II *Acaena microphylla*
III *Malva moschata* · Musk mallow   IV *Primula* sp.   V *Hypericum* sp.(?)

II
Bocconia cordata
Plume Poppy

I

I *Veronica longifolia*   **II** *Bocconia cordata* · Plume poppy

The importance of feeding is now widely recognized and the low nutrient content of manures and composts generally appreciated. For rosarians such as Dean Hole, the distinction between soil amendments and fertilizers was evidently blurred, and it is hard to see why he minimized the value of bone meal which, with its high phosphate content, makes an excellent pre-planting base dressing. For the continued vitality of the rose, a twice-yearly application (at the start of growth in the spring and then after the first flush of flowers) of a modern, specially formulated rose fertilizer is essential. Although many an expert rose grower will probably (and, a century ago would certainly) tell you that each and every type of rose, not to say individual variety, requires a different feeding regime, more than adequate plants will be obtained with this overall guideline. And so much simpler it is than the varied blends of pigeon guano, soot, leaves, liquid extract of horse droppings, night soil, pond water, brewers' waste, bone extracts, peat, charcoal, pig dung, wood ashes, nitrate of soda, saltpetre or blood – all, among others, advocated by various Victorian rosarians.

Yet, whereas roses may grow well with correct and balanced feeding, their continued health and vitality will only come from careful attention to pest and disease control. The fungal diseases – black spot and mildew – together with insect pests – most notably greenfly – have been problems for as long as roses have been cultivated, although the relative importance of black spot is now much greater, for two reasons. First, susceptibility to black spot in roses is clearly associated with the genes for yellow colour, and the obsession since the end of the last century with yellow roses has resulted in a much greater general incidence of the problem. Second, the passing in this century of legislation restricting the emissions of sulphurous fumes from factory chimneys has removed an atmospheric fungicide that helped to keep the incidence of black spot in Victorian gardens to less dramatic proportions.

SULPHUR, SOOT AND NICOTINE

Mildew was then the more serious concern and the most widely used remedies were sulphur or soot, both of moderate effectiveness, whilst the insect pests were usually combated with dilute nicotine (tobacco water) or extract of quassia. For the more organically inclined gardeners, sulphur and quassia (or an alternative plant derivative, derris) are still reliable as fungicide and insecticide respectively, although a modern proprietary blend of a systemic fungicide such as triforine, the non-systemic fungicide bupirimate and the specific aphicide pirimicarb, will almost certainly give better and longer-lasting protection.

A large proportion of the modern rose gardener's manual will be devoted to the subject of pruning, for this has become a matter of importance with modern roses far greater than is the case with any other garden shrub. Very largely this is because the present day large- and cluster-flowered roses decline swiftly into feeble flowered shadows unless carefully and assiduously pruned each year. Pruning was much less of a preoccupation for the Victorian rose grower who was able to treat the majority of his plants as he treated many other flowering shrubs. His concern was merely to remove sufficient growth to maintain an appropriate proportion of new and old wood, to prevent overcrowding of shoots, to get rid of diseased material, to snip off dead heads of those varieties that would not later grace the garden with autumn hips and, of course, to cut back in October by about one-quarter all those long shoots that would otherwise be whipped by the winter winds and render the plants unstable.

Pruning of most roses would be completed in March, although the slightly less hardy Teas,

The rose has always been subject to more than its fair share of pests. The leaf-rolling sawfly shown here was always a major concern to nineteenth-century gardeners although they were fortunate in that the modern scourge of blackspot was rarely serious.

Noisettes and Bourbons would be left until April. These precepts applied equally to shrubs, climbers and, in more restricted fashion, to standards. The Victorian standard rose played an important part in the formal rose gardens or rosaries of the time, although, predictably, they came to be abhorred by those of Robinsonian persuasion who considered few things to have had a worse influence on the flower garden than the standard rose on the top of its 'ugly stick'. This was, however, only partly an aesthetic objection for most considered a well-grown standard to be appealing. The problem, as often as not, was the unsuitability of the rose variety used for rootstock.

Roses are grafted or budded onto rootstocks largely for reasons of expediency on the part of nurserymen who thus derive many plants from a single short length of budwood, and obtain marketable plants within a season. Today, the rootstocks generally used are the species *Rosa coriifolia froebelii*, usually called *Rosa laxa*, or the more strongly rooting *Rosa multiflora*. Both have the advantage of suckering less than English briar, the dog rose, *Rosa canina*, used widely in the early part of this century and before. For the Victorian gardener, however, another rootstock, an Italian form of Noisette rose called Manetti, was also used extensively, but was nonetheless roundly cursed by many gardeners of the time. Although plants on Manetti stock were claimed to establish and flower more quickly, it was generally found inferior to English briar, especially for Tea roses. Inevitably, it was William Robinson, never a man to mince his words, who actually published the wish that Signor Manetti had never been born. And in common with many other Victorian gardeners, he expressed his support for the view (now again becoming fashionable) that roses grown on their own roots have many advantages, not least in their absence of suckering. Some gardeners of the period even went so far as to advocate the striking of rose cuttings in the position in which they would ultimately be grown on to flower – rather than raising them first in a 'cutting bed'.

By the latter part of the Victorian period, William Robinson was advocating a mixture of roses with other types of plant, an attractive blend that even today is scarcely appreciated.

CHAPTER VIII

SHRUBS IN THE VICTORIAN GARDEN

THE ORNAMENTAL shrub is arguably the most important feature of the modern garden. It certainly exemplifies to perfection the minimal maintenance characteristics that so many late twentieth-century home gardeners require of their plants. The shrub is semi-permanent, demanding only a good soil and thorough soil preparation before planting, a modicum of annual feeding (although many, probably the majority, are denied even this, yet thrive) and, in some cases, a modicum of annual pruning (which, again, many are denied). In return, shrubs offer a wide range of attractions, achieving their ornamental appeal through massed blossom or individual flowers, perfume, foliage colour or shape, bark colour or texture, or simply overall form and shape of the plant. Many have the important additional feature of retaining their leaves throughout the year.

Yet shrubs, in the modern sense of the term, are relative newcomers to British gardens. One reason is that most modern gardeners grow the majority of their shrubs in mixture with herbaceous perennials and, to some degree, with bedding plants too, in what has become known as the mixed border. As I explained in Chapter VI, this development from the Victorian herbaceous border has occurred recently in reaction to the dictates of modern gardening life. Such a procedure would have been relatively unfamiliar to the Victorians.

Perhaps the most important difference, however, between Victorian and modern-day shrub cultivation relates to the range of available species. A good average garden centre today will stock perhaps 200 different types, a specialist nursery several thousand. Yet reference to a Victorian catalogue will reveal many fewer, for two main reasons. As I mentioned in Chapter II, many of the most desirable and popular of modern-day garden shrub species were nineteenth-century introductions to Britain, and even by the end of the period had not proved themselves sufficiently amenable to rapid and large scale propagation for nurserymen to be able to offer them freely. But perhaps more significantly still, the range of *varieties*, as opposed to species, was even more restricted. Because of their relatively slow growth and maturation, the deliberate hybridization and selection of woody plants is a much more tedious and lengthy process than it is with annuals or herbaceous perennials. Hence a large proportion of the shrub varieties that we grow today arose originally as genetic mutants or sports rather than as the result of deliberate and concerted breeding effort, and are perpetuated by cuttings rather than through the medium of seeds. Yet the laws of chance dictate that the longer and more widely the original species is cultivated, the greater is the likelihood of sports arising, being detected and capitalized upon. Only after several decades

Kerria Japonica

I *Prunus* sp. · Plum   **II** *Malus* sp. · Apple
III *Kerria japonica* · Single Jew's mallow   **IV** *Cystisus* sp. · Broom

are there likely to be many horticulturally desirable varieties. But this throws up another point too, for the modern garden is generally small – less than 200 sq. m (about 2,000 sq. ft) on average; and for a plant to be horticulturally desirable in such an environment it must also be fairly small. Thus, nurserymen in recent times have tended to concentrate on selecting the sports or new varieties that are inherently lower growing and more compact than those of 100 years ago when space was less limiting. The so-called dwarf variety is one of the hallmarks of the modern home garden.

There is one other important consideration. The larger the plant, the less likely it is, as a rule, that nurserymen will trouble to continue cultivating a form or variety that no longer has much horticultural appeal. Thus it is often hard to obtain authentically old varieties of shrubs from nurseries, although conversely, because the individual plants are fairly long-lived, it is more likely than in the case of herbaceous perennials or bedding annuals that the old forms still exist in old gardens.

COMPARATIVE LISTS

The contrast between the modern and the Victorian gardeners' shrub selection is well illustrated by the following two lists. The first was published in a British gardening magazine in 1893 in response to a reader's request for the names of 'the two dozen best evergreen shrubs'. I have added modern names in brackets where these differ and the plants' origins and dates of introduction to Britain:

Andromeda polifolia (Native)
Aucuba japonica (Japan, 1793)
Berberis aquifolium (= *Mahonia aquifolium*; W. North
  America, 1823)
Berberis darwinii (Chile, 1849)
Berberis stenophylla (= *B.* × *stenophylla*; Nursery origin,
  1860)
Buxus balearica (Balearic Islands, S. Spain, 1780)
Buxus sempervirens (Native)
Common laurel (*Prunus laurocerasus*; S.E. Europe, early
  17th century)
Portugal laurel (*Prunus lusitanica*; Spain and Portugal,
  before 1648)
Cotoneaster microphyllus (Himalayas, W. China, 1824)
Euonymus fortunei var. *radicans* (Japan, ?)

The Victorian shrubbery *is often thought of as a somewhat dull feature, populated by relatively dull plants such as* Garrya elliptica *and laurel. Nonetheless, in the correct setting, as in this rectory garden at Eversley, the combination of different leaf shapes and shades of green can be very pleasing.*

Euonymus japonicus (Japan, 1804)
Evergreen oak (presumably Holm Oak, *Quercus ilex*; Mediterranean, before 16th century)
Garrya elliptica (W. North America, 1828)
Golden holly (an *Ilex aquifolium* cultivar; Native, cv. ancient)
Hypericum calycinum (S.E. Europe, 1676)
Laurustinus (*Viburnum tinus*; Mediterranean region, 16th century)
Olearia haastii (= *O.* × *haastii*; New Zealand, 1858)
Oval-leaved privet (*Ligustrum ovalifolium*; Japan, 1885)
Phillyrea angustifolia (Mediterranean region, before 1597)
Rhododendron ponticum (Naturalized from S.E. Europe/W. Asia, late 17th century)
Silver Queen holly (*Ilex aquifolium* 'Silver Queen', ?)
Skimmia japonica (Japan and surrounding area, 1838)
Sweet bay (*Laurus nobilis*; Mediterranean region, before 16th century)

This is a typical late Victorian selection, but it includes one large tree (*Quercus ilex*); two large and rampant shrubs that most gardeners today would class almost as weeds (*Rhododendron ponticum* and *Hypericum calycinum*); three plants which, although attractive and useful, find their greatest merit in seaside areas (*Euonymus japonicus*, *Phillyrea angustifolia* and *Olearia haastii*); two plants grown essentially as hedging subjects, and even then with serious drawbacks (*Prunus laurocerasus* and *Ligustrum ovalifolium*); one plant which, although valuable, is somewhat tender (*Laurus nobilis*); and one plant, although desirable, which is restricted to very acid soils (*Andromeda polifolia*). This leaves 14 shrubs that are still widely grown today. All are still available as the basic types, although in several instances the modern gardener would choose a more recent and better variety – e.g. *Mahonia aquifolium* 'Apollo' or *Garrya elliptica* 'James Roof'.

By comparison, the following list appeared in 1983 as a result of a survey of British garden centres for their best and most popular shrubs for typical (and therefore fairly small) gardens. Again, I have added their origins and the dates (if known) when each was introduced to Britain. (It is noticeable how few plants here are grown as true species; most are either natural varieties (var.) or cultivars (cv.)

– varieties that have arisen in cultivation, either deliberately through hybridization or accidentally.

Acer palmatum dissectum atropurpureum (Species Japan, 1820; var. ?)
Aucuba japonica 'Variegata' (Japan, 1793)
Berberis thunbergii 'Rose Glow' (Species China, Japan, c. 1874; cv. 1957)
Ceratostigma willmottianum (China, 1908)
Chaenomeles × *superba* 'Crimson and Gold' (Hybrid nursery origin, late 19th century; cv. 1939)
Chamaecyparis pisifera 'Boulevard' (Species Japan, 1861; cv. c. 1934)
Cotoneaster horizontalis (China, c. 1870)
Daphne mezereum (Native)
Elaeagnus pungens 'Maculata' (Species Japan, 1830; cv. late 19th century)
Euonymus fortunei 'Emerald 'n' Gold' (Species E. Asia c. 1865; cv. late 20th century)
Forsythia × *intermedia* 'Lynwood' (Hybrid nursery origin c. 1900; cv. 1935)
Hamamelis mollis 'Pallida' (Species China 1879; cv. 20th century)
Hebe × *franciscana* (Hybrid garden origin, late 19th century?)
Hypericum 'Hidcote' (? 20th century)
Philadelphus coronarius 'Aureus' (Species S.E. Europe/W. Asia, before 16th century; cv. ?)
Potentilla 'Red Ace' (cv. late 20th century)
Skimmia japonica 'Rubella' (Species China 1838; cv. late 20th century)
Spiraea × *arguta* (Hybrid nursery origin, before 1884)
Viburnum farreri (China, 1910)
Weigela 'Bristol Ruby' (Hybrid nursery origin, late 19th century; cv. 20th century)

Remember, moreover, that this is a list for the average small modern garden. Larger gardens could be expected to include *Buddleia davidii* (1890), *Caryopteris* × *clandonensis* (20th century), *Hydrangea* 'Blue Wave' (c. 1900), and ornamental trees such as the cherry 'Kanzan' (1913), *Laburnum* × *wateri* 'Vossii' (late 19th century), *Robinia pseudoacacia* 'Frisia' (1935) and *Sorbus* 'Joseph Rock' (1932), all of which were either unavailable or not freely obtainable in the late nineteenth century.

The conclusion, therefore, is that perhaps 25 per cent of a representative sample of shrubs likely to be found in a British garden centre today could authentically have been seen in a late Victorian British garden, while perhaps a further 25 per cent

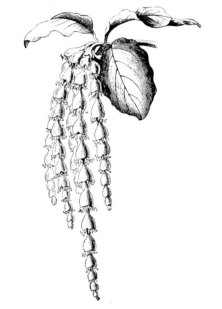

Garrya elliptica *was introduced to Britain from North America by David Douglas in 1828 and soon attained popularity for its green winter catkins.*

Rhododendron Dauricum
(Daurian Rhododendron)

Viburnum tinus
(Laurestinus)

Scilla Sibirica
(Siberian
Squill)

Galanthus elwesi
(elwesi
snowdrop)

Leucojum vernum
(Spring Snowflake)

Dondia
Epipactis

Pernettya

I   *Scilla siberica* · Siberian or Spring squill   II   *Hacquetia (= Dondia) epipactis*   III   *Leucojum vernum* · Spring snowflake
IV   *Rhododendron dauricum* · Daurian rhododendron   V   *Galanthus elwesii* · Snowdrop   VI   *Viburnum tinus* · Laurustinus
VII   *Pernettya* sp.   VIII   *Primula elatior* · Oxlip

I *Rhododendron* sp.   II *Omphalodes verna* · Blue-eye Mary
III *Galanthus nivalis* 'Flore Pleno'· *Double snowdrop*

are modern varieties of species that might have been used in their original form (which may now be very hard to obtain). Further suggestions for Victorian shrubs are included in the Directory of Plants.

HEDGES AND TOPIARY

I would now like to consider more closely two special uses of shrubs in gardens – hedges and topiary. Hedges are simply shrubs planted in rows and clipped to maintain predetermined height and width. They have been used for centuries both as garden boundaries and for providing internal divisions within the garden. The types of shrub that are suitable for hedging must be amenable to this form of training, capable of forming a barrier solid enough to provide wind protection, and flexible enough not to be damaged by winter gales. They must also, when used as garden boundaries, be sufficiently robust to exclude intruders, and although this would once have meant cattle and horses, it is now more likely to mean the neighbour's dog.

Of the plants suitable for and in sympathy with the Victorian garden, one must surely surpass all others. Yew really is the perfect hedging plant, forming a truly beautiful wall of green, perhaps a little slow to establish but not, as often believed, a slow grower. Alternatives, especially as boundaries rather than structural features, are beech and holly. The ubiquitous and unutterably dismal Japanese privet – which was introduced to Britain at the end of the nineteenth century and found favour in the first half of the present century, principally because of its tolerance of pollution in towns – can justifiably be excluded. Apart from its singularly unattractive appearance, it requires more trimming than almost any other type of hedging shrub. Ideally, hedges should be cut two or even three times during a season, although most can be cut once only and not appear too unkempt. Privet is an exception, and if cut less than twice will soon be well on the way to forming neither hedge nor shrub, but a tree. The common laurel, *Prunus laurocerasus*, was probably second in popularity to privet for hedging at the end of the last century

but it has one important drawback – its very big leaves. If cut with shears, these leaves are inevitably sliced, look unsightly, and often brown and wither in consequence of the treatment. Over the past ten or so years, the once predominant place of privet has been taken by fast-growing conifers, especially the hybrid Leyland cypress. This can have no place in a Victorian style of garden for it did not exist until it arose as a chance hybrid at the end of the Victorian period and was not used for hedging until well into this century. Lawson cypress was introduced to Britain from western North America in 1854 but it was several years before it became widely available and popular as a hedging plant. However, it is interesting to note that many of the present vast range of forms and varieties did, in fact, begin to appear before the end of the nineteenth century, indicative of a highly unstable and plastic genetic constitution. The Monterey cypress, *Cupressus macrocarpa*, which preceded Leyland cypress as a popular large hedging plant in the middle years of this century, was introduced earlier than Lawson, around Queen Victoria's coronation year, but it was not used widely in the nineteenth century other than as a specimen tree.

There is one other conifer that could, indeed should, authentically find a place in the large Victorian-style flower garden as a specimen plant. If ever a single tree can be said to epitomize Victoria's reign, it was the bizarre and unlovely monkey puzzle, *Araucaria araucana*, introduced to Britain from South America by Archibald Menzies in 1795 and again and more significantly by William Lobb in 1844. It can justifiably be excluded from small gardens by its ultimate size – about 30 m (100 ft) – and it is unfortunate that in their enthusiasm for this tree, the Victorians were not more aware of its growth potential. Many examples still exist in small town gardens where

Birds are among the most commonly seen topiary features and are probably easier to shape than most other forms of living subject.

Patience and a very complicated metal framework are needed to create topiary pictures such as this old English bear-baiting scene.

TOPIARY

The shaping of trees and shrubs into sculptural forms dates back around two thousand years. Over the centuries, there seems scarcely any type of evergreen shrub that has not been used for topiary at some time, but large-leaved species such as laurel are not very suitable. During the eighteenth century in Britain, topiary declined in popularity and this explains why there are so few ancient examples still extant. Nonetheless, some did survive, curiously enough, in the larger cottage gardens and during the early nineteenth century these provided the inspiration for a quite remarkable revival of the art. This time, it tended to be yew that predominated and in a temperate climate, this is certainly the most suitable subject.

The finest examples of British topiary are probably those at Levens Hall in Cumbria (right), although there are also some fine specimens in yew and holly in the old Drummond family residence of Megginch Castle, including a splendid crown planted to celebrate Queen Victoria's diamond jubilee in 1897.

they dominate both house and neighbourhood, and also display a general dislike of an industrial atmosphere by lacking many of their branches. In addition to its overall size, the monkey puzzle also has the attribute of being virtually unprunable.

Topiary is the training and pruning of shrubs into complex and more or less sculptural shapes. It is an ancient art; the Roman word for a gardener was in fact *topiarius*, and topiary, even in its modern sense, was well known to the Romans. Throughout subsequent periods of gardening history, topiary played an important role. It is therefore not uniquely characteristic of the nineteenth century, although two or three examples would sit comfortably in such a garden environment. To respond well to topiary, a shrub must be evergreen, small-leaved, of generally dense habit and reasonably slow growing. The early Roman topiarists used the Italian cypress (*Cupressus sempervirens*), but far and away the best and most

successful topiary in the British Isles has been achieved with yew. Small-leaved box is probably the best second choice, although examples also exist of holly and other evergreens.

While time and labour constraints mean that large topiary specimens must today be cut with powered trimmers, a good pair of shears certainly gives the best and most controlled cutting for small garden examples. The complex and inherently unstable shapes such as swan-necked birds are always formed around a stout metal framework, but for the small garden it is perhaps more sensible to concentrate on self-supporting topiary such as ball or pyramid forms. One additional word of advice must be offered as a result of anguished personal experience. Always create each item of topiary as an individual specimen. If there is a harder and more frustrating gardening task than attempting to shape a matching pair of topiary shrubs, I have yet to find it.

CHAPTER IX

A DIRECTORY OF PLANTS

The plants listed here include most of those depicted on Alice Drummond-Hay's paintings, together with a selection of other Victorian types that were apparently not grown at Seggieden. An indication is given of some of those old cultivars known still to exist and, more particularly, of those listed in accessible catalogues, but no attempt has been made to be comprehensive and I have not scoured the catalogues of small nurseries nor lists of private collections. I hope, however, that by publishing this information, nurseries and private individuals with authentically old cultivars not mentioned will be prompted to come forward and make them more generally available. The objective here is simply to give sufficient guidance to enable a representative few of each species to be chosen, although for many of the more popular plants, including carnations, chrysanthemums, daffodils, dahlias, delphiniums, gladioli, violas and pansies, there are specialist societies who may well have more detailed lists of information. Such societies may also maintain registers of small, specialist nurseries with old varieties.

The plants are arranged alphabetically under their scientific generic names although in each case I have also given the British common names if these exist. I have used abbreviations to indicate the type of plant in each genus as follows: HA – hardy annual; HB – hardy biennial; HP – hardy perennial; HHA – half-hardy annual; S – shrub and T – tree (with the additional designation in the latter two of d – dwarf, s – small, m – medium or l – large). Page references are to Alice Drummond-Hay's paintings.

Achillea millefolium
'Rosea' (Rosy yarrow)

A

ACAENA Rosaceae
ROCK GARDEN, MODERATELY SHADE TOLERANT GROUND COVER **HP**

Compact carpeting plants, useful for covering large areas with their densely packed, usually bronze-green leaves. The red, almost burr-like flowers are curious if not beautiful from late autumn until well into the winter. There are some modern cultivars but the New Zealand species *A. microphylla* was formerly popular. Available from seed or as plants. 8cm/3in. PAGE 80.

ACHILLEA Compositae
HERBACEOUS BORDER, ROCK GARDEN **HP**

Milfoils A large genus with some fine modern cultivars but the old coloured-leaved forms 'Roseum' or 'Purpureum' of the native species *A. millefolium* are useful if undistinguished plants for the herbaceous border. They were also used as rough 'lawn' plants, especially on dry slopes. *A. tomentosa* is a useful mat-forming species with dense woolly leaves for the front of the border or rock garden. Seed or plants. 5cm-1.2m/2in-4ft.

Chelidonium majus
(Celandine)

I

IV

III

II

Phlox subulata
(Moss Pink)

VI

V

Primula cortusoides amoena
(Sieboldi).

I *Chelidonium majus* · Greater celandine   **II** *Phlox subulata*
III *Daboecia cantabrica* · St Dabeoc's heath   **IV** *Fuchsia* sp.
V *Primula cortusoides*   **VI** Unidentified

ACONITUM Ranunculaceae
HERBACEOUS BORDER **HP**

Monkshood A few species have always been important and distinctively beautiful mid-border species, although the tuberous roots are poisonous. Avoid selected modern forms and choose the deep bluish purple species *A. napellus*, although this name is used to cover a range of related types. Seed or plants. 1-1.2m/3-4ft.

ADONIS Ranunculaceae
HERBACEOUS BORDER, ROCK GARDEN **HA/HP**

Pheasant's Eyes Almost like a cross between an anemone and a buttercup with feathery foliage. Lovely in the border; *A. vernalis*, yellow in spring, is the old perennial cottage favourite but *A. aestivalis* is a smaller red-flowered summer annual. *A. pyrenaica* is a yellow alpine species for the rock garden. Seed or plants. 20-40cm/8-16in.

AGAPANTHUS Liliaceae
HERBACEOUS BORDER **HP**

African Blue Lilies Impressive clump-forming South African plants for well drained soils and warm sunny and sheltered sites. They produce large clusters of blue, almost lily-like flowers in late summer and are usually referred to in Victorian books and catalogues as *A. umbellatus* although all 'species' are probably hybrids. The modern Headbourne Hybrids are among the best, but for older types choose 'Mixed Species' or *A. campanulatus*. Seed, bulbs or plants. 40-70cm/16-28in.

AGERATUM Compositae
BEDDING **HHA/HA**

Invaluable for all types of bedding; especially the types with closely packed masses of small, rather feathery blue flowers. The commonest of the old species was *A. mexicanum*, now usually called *A. houstonianum*. It is all but ousted today by modern dwarf selections and F$_1$ hybrids. Closest to the old taller form is probably 'Blue Bouquet' but the old dwarfs such as 'Tom Thumb' and 'Imperial Dwarf' seem to have vanished; 'Blue Mink' could substitute. Seed. 20-45cm/8-18in.

AGROSTEMMA Caryophyllaceae
HERBACEOUS BORDER **HB/HP**

Rose Campion *Agrostemma coronaria*, with feathery-woolly foliage and single crimson flowers (although white and double forms also occur), is among the apparently lost garden flowers although in fact still freely available. It is not, however, reliably perennial in all gardens. Seed. 60cm/2ft.

ALCEA Malvaceae
HERBACEOUS BORDER **HP**

Hollyhock Perhaps most people's idea of the classic cottage garden plant, the hollyhock has been a part of English gardening since the late sixteenth century. A Victorian garden without hollyhocks is unthinkable, and the rust disease that disfigures the foliage can partially be avoided by modern fungicides. Many dozens of cultivars have come and gone and modern seed catalogues offer depressing modern mixtures. These must suffice, but avoid the dwarf 'Majorette' types which would be quite inappropriate. Seed. 1.5-2m/5-6ft.

ALLIUM Liliaceae
ROCK GARDEN, HERBACEOUS BORDER **HP**

Ornamental Onions Far more species are grown and are freely available today than were used in the Victorian garden, but a place should be found for the small, yellow-flowered *A. moly* (12-25cm/5-10in), which can be slightly invasive given free rein and the taller, blue *A. caeruleum*. Bulbs. 20-80cm/8in-2ft 8in.

ALONSOA Scrophulariaceae
BEDDING **HHA**

Mask Flower Alonsoas are among the almost forgotten bedding plants, although some catalogues still list seed of *A. warscewiczii* (despite its name, a South American). This is a small, shrubby plant with red-brown shoots and clusters of rather large red flowers. Grow it as a half-hardy annual and consider it as representative of its kind for other formerly cultivated species seem to be unobtainable. Seed. 60cm/2ft.

Flower-stem and root of
Aconitum napellus
(Monkshood, Wolf's bane)

Amaranthus caudatus
(Love-lies-bleeding)

ALSTROEMERIA Liliaceae
HERBACEOUS BORDER, SHADE GARDEN **HP**

Peruvian Lilies (sometimes formerly called **Chilean Lilies**) Lily-like flowers in a range of colours; may need slight protection until well established. Today, hybrids of *A. ligtu* and *A. haemantha* are the most widely grown, but *A. aurea* (also called *A. aurantiaca*) – up to 1m/3ft – with large orange-yellow flowers would be more typical of the nineteenth century. Seed or bulbs.

ALTERNANTHERA Amaranthaceae
BEDDING **HHA**

Predominantly tropical American perennials with variously coloured leaves, once very important as foliage plants in bedding schemes because of their amenability to being clipped to maintain a neat habit. Most of the popular old types such as *magnifica* and *paronychioides* were forms of the Brazilian *A. bettzichiana*, but they are now very scarce and seem to have disappeared from catalogues. Seed. 2-8cm/1-3in (aided by clipping).

ALYSSUM Cruciferae
FRONT OF HERBACEOUS BORDER **HA**

Rock Madwort The modern bedding alyssums like 'Little Dorrit' are forms of *Lobularia maritima* (7-8cm/3in) but in Victorian gardens alyssum usually meant the taller, golden yellow, spring-flowering *A. saxatile* (20-30cm/8-12in) of which Hibberd said it was impossible to have too much. The original species is a straggly plant and 'Compactum' (10-15cm/4-6in) is much neater. Seed. PAGE 20.

AMARANTHUS Amaranthaceae
BEDDING **HHA/HA**

Taller species like Love-lies-bleeding, *A. caudatus* (60-100cm/2-3ft), with long, drooping tail-like red flower heads were used as feature plants in bedding schemes, but forms of a plant called *A. gangeticus*, especially the one known as *melancholicus*, were more generally grown in bedding for their coloured leaves. Modern catalogues list cultivars of the same species and call it *A. tricolor*. Seed.

ANEMONE Ranunculaceae
ROCK GARDEN, HERBACEOUS BORDER **HP**

Three main groups were, and are, important. In the rock garden, species such as *A. nemorosa*, *A. appenina* and *A. hepatica* or *triloba* (now usually called *Hepatica nobilis*), together with the closely related pulsatillas, are invaluable little early season flowers (10-15cm/4-6in) in a range of colours. In the herbaceous border *A. japonica* (= *A.* × *hybrida*) has long been an invaluable plant of late autumn. It occurs in various colour forms although none is better than the old white 'Honorine Jobert'. At the front of the border, forms of the poppy anemone *A. coronaria* (30cm/1ft) were as popular as Victorian cut flowers as they are today. The French 'De Caen' were, and still are, the most widely grown. Seed, corms or plants. PAGES 16, 20, 77, 96, 117, 125, 132.

ANTIRRHINUM Scrophulariaceae
BEDDING, HERBACEOUS BORDER **HHA**

Snapdragons Cultivars of *A. majus* have declined slightly in popularity in recent years but the Victorians knew their worth. They are extremely easy to grow but should be sown early for best results. Avoid the too floriferous modern F_1 and F_2 hybrids and dwarfs, and look instead for taller types. It is doubtful if true nineteenth-century cultivars are still to be found, having succumbed to rust and virus diseases, but the modern 'Monarch' range (about 40cm/16in) have some resistance to rust. Seed. PAGE 100.

AQUILEGIA Ranunculaceae
HERBACEOUS BORDER **HP**

Columbines Although there are many delightful dwarf and small species, like the stunning *A. canadensis* which grew at Seggieden, it is the many double and variously coloured forms of the common *A. vulgaris* that so evoke the Victorian garden in early summer and which are usually called 'Granny's Bonnets'. The old types can be bought as *A. vulgaris* and *A. vulgaris* 'Flore Pleno'. An apparently old and unusually appealing cultivar with double green and pink flowers that comes more or less true from seed is now called 'Nora Barlow'. Seed or plants. 60-110cm/2ft-3ft 6in. PAGE 25.

Alcea rosea
(Double hollyhock)

Anemone Hepatica
(coerulea (blue) & Triloba
- rubra (pink)

I *Primula vulgaris* · Primrose   II *Vinca* sp. · Periwinkle
III *Hepatica nobilis (= Hepatica rubra = Anemone triloba)*
IV *Mahonia aquifolium* · Oregon grape

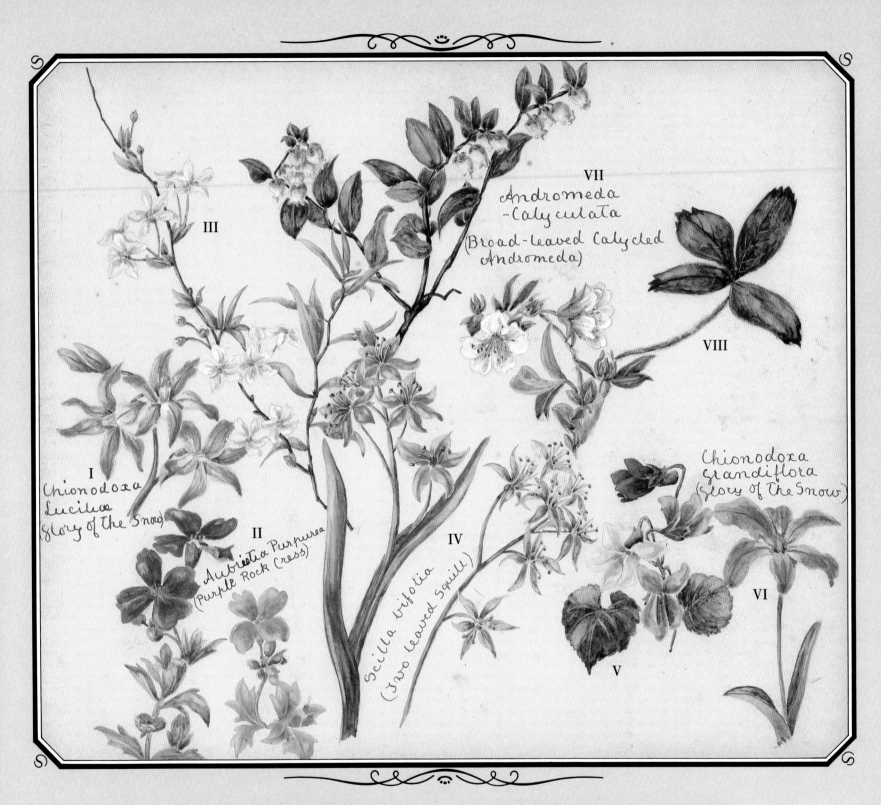

I *Chionodoxa luciliae* · Glory of the snow   II *Aubrieta purpurea* · Purple aubretia   III Unidentified

IV *Scilla bifolia* · Squill   V *Viola* sp. (probably *V. odorata*) · Violet

VI *Ipheion uniflorum*   VII *Chamaedaphne (= Andromeda) calyculata*   VIII Unidentified

ARABIS Cruciferae
ROCK GARDEN, WALLS, FRONT OF HERBACEOUS BORDER **HP**

Rock Cress 'Snow Cap' and 'Snow White' are typical modern forms of *A. albida*, but cultivars are also available of the pink *A. blepharophylla*, rather less hardy but another Victorian favourite. 'Compinkie' is a modern mat-forming pink plant, not authentically of old form. Seed or plants. 7-15cm/3-6in. PAGES 16, 77.

ARMERIA Plumbaginaceae
ROCK GARDEN, WALLS **HP**

Thrift A much loved spring-flowering, cushion-forming plant, as well known in Britain in the wild on sea cliffs as in the garden. White and red as well as pink forms exist, and the modern forms are perfectly acceptable. 'Laucheana' is the excellent strong-growing, old deep pink form, still available. Seed or plants. 15cm/6in.

Bouvardia jasminiflora

ARNEBIA Boraginaceae
ROCK GARDEN, FRONT OF HERBACEOUS BORDER **HP**

Prophet Flower Often called *Echioides longiflora* today. A coarse-leaved relative of borage, with unusually attractive deep yellow trumpet flowers in late spring, bearing five purple spots. Apparently very scarce today. Seed or plants. 25-30cm/10-12in. PAGE 117.

ASTER Compositae
HERBACEOUS BORDER **HP**

Michaelmas Daisies, formerly called **Starworts** There are modern tall cultivars with some resistance to mildew, but authentically old types will always give trouble and although associated with cottage gardens, even the Victorian gardeners recognized their defects and never rated them highly. The best to use are the smaller forms of *A. amellus* (about 60cm/2ft) which was grown widely in the nineteenth century. Plants. PAGES 104, 105, 120, 124, 129.

ASTRANTIA Umbelliferae
HERBACEOUS BORDER **HP**

Masterwort Rather few members of the huge family Umbelliferae have achieved importance in the flower garden but astrantias are notable exceptions. *A. major* (60cm/2ft) and *A. minor* have been cultivated for several hundred years and their long-lasting blooms are as valuable in dried flower decorations as they are in the border. There is a variegated form of *A. minor* (25cm/10in) which seems to be old. They all appreciate light shade. Seed or plants.

AUBRIETA Cruciferae
ROCK GARDEN, FRONT OF HERBACEOUS BORDER **HP**

Purple Rock Cress Indispensable today for spring colour and long grown in gardens. Most of the old named cultivars seem to have vanished in favour of F_1 hybrids and modern hybrid mixtures. Choose any named cultivars available and include *A. deltoides* 'Variegata' which may be the same as the old variegated foliage form so praised by the Victorians. Seed or plants. 6-8cm/2-3in. PAGES 97, 109.

—*B*—

BEGONIA Begoniaceae
BEDDING **HHA**

Although begonias are now indispensable parts of the pattern of summer bedding, it should be realized that they were late-comers to the scene. The basis of the modern tuberous begonia lies with the various South American species introduced principally by the Veitch nursery in the latter years of the last century. The modern tuberous hybrids have changed almost beyond recognition from these early forms and would be quite out of keeping in a Victorian setting. The fibrous-rooted bedding begonias of today are derived from *B. semperflorens*, originally introduced to Britain from Brazil in 1829 and extensively selected and hybridized. Those F_1 and other hybrids available today, however, bear very little resemblance to them.

BELLIS Compositae
FRONT OF HERBACEOUS BORDER, PERENNIAL BEDDING **HP**

Daisy Although this is the same species, *B. perennis*, that most gardeners seek to eradicate from their lawns, the double forms are desirable. Most of the old named types have disappeared, but choose any named individual colour forms; 'Dresden China' is perhaps the best double pink. Seed or plants. 6-8cm/2-3in. PAGE 17.

BERBERIS Berberidaceae
SHRUBBERY S (s-m)

Berberis darwinii, brought back from South America by William Lobb in 1849, has been called the finest flowering shrub ever introduced to British gardening. It should certainly be one of the glories of the spring shrubbery, where it could usefully be joined by *B.* × *stenophylla*, a hybrid between *B. darwinii* and *B. empetrifolia* which appeared in a nursery around 1860, and *B. thunbergii*, an Oriental species introduced about four years later. But be certain to obtain the species, for the garden market today is flooded with twentieth-century hybrids. Plants. 3.5m/12ft. PAGE 53.

BOCCONIA Papaveraceae
HERBACEOUS BORDER HP

Plume Poppy Huge shrubby perennials with heart-shaped leaves, sometimes called Tree Celandines. They are rather like very tall Greater Celandines, with masses of creamy flowers throughout the summer, and are valuable at the back of a large border. The most popular species was *B. cordata*, now usually called *Macleaya cordata*. Seed or plants. 2-3m/7-10ft. PAGE 81.

BOUVARDIA Rubiaceae
BEDDING HHA

Although usually seen today, if at all, as greenhouse plants, these were used extensively in the nineteenth century as half-hardy bedding by stopping them to produce a bushy habit. They have striking red flowers, rather like large, bright red, pink or white Bedstraws (to which they are related) and their late autumn flowering (which extends into winter under cover) rendered them valuable for 'out of season' buttonholes and bouquets. There were many named hybrid cultivars but most seem to have vanished from seed catalogues in recent years and will need searching for. Seed. 20-30cm/8-12in (by stopping).

BUDDLEIA Loganiaceae
SHRUBBERY S (m)

The popular modern buddleias are forms of *B. davidii* which is virtually post-Victorian, the seed from which present-day forms are derived having been introduced to Britain from China in the years after 1900. Buddleia in the nineteenth century meant the South American Orange Ball Tree, *B. globosa*, a rather gaunt straggly plant, and slightly tender too but with interesting flowers and well worth a place in the larger garden. Plants. 2-3m/9-10ft. PAGE 45.

BULBOCODIUM Liliaceae
ROCK GARDEN, FRONT OF HERBACEOUS BORDER HP

Bulbocodium vernum is a valuable early spring plant with tubular reddish purple flowers on short stems from March onwards, its flowering season usually overlapping attractively with late snowdrops. The true species is freely available. Corms. 8-15cm/ 3-6in. PAGE 108.

CALANDRINIA Portulacaceae
BEDDING HHA

The bright red-flowered South American *C. umbellata* can still be found in seed catalogues but it is a relative rarity now compared with its former importance as a bedding plant. Nonetheless, it would be highly appropriate for the Victorian garden and likely to succeed best in a sunny, well drained situation. Although hardy enough to be treated as a biennial in favoured areas, this is risky and it is best sown under protection as a half-hardy annual. Seed. 15cm/6in.

CALCEOLARIA Scrophulariaceae
BEDDING HHA

Slipper Flower This is a very large genus although few species are seen commonly. The hideously coloured, large-flowered, herbaceous pot calceolarias so popular today are usually called *C.* × *herbeohybrida*. The modern bedding calceolarias such as 'Sunshine' are F_1 and other hybrids of the shrubby *C. rugosa* that

Calandrinia umbellata

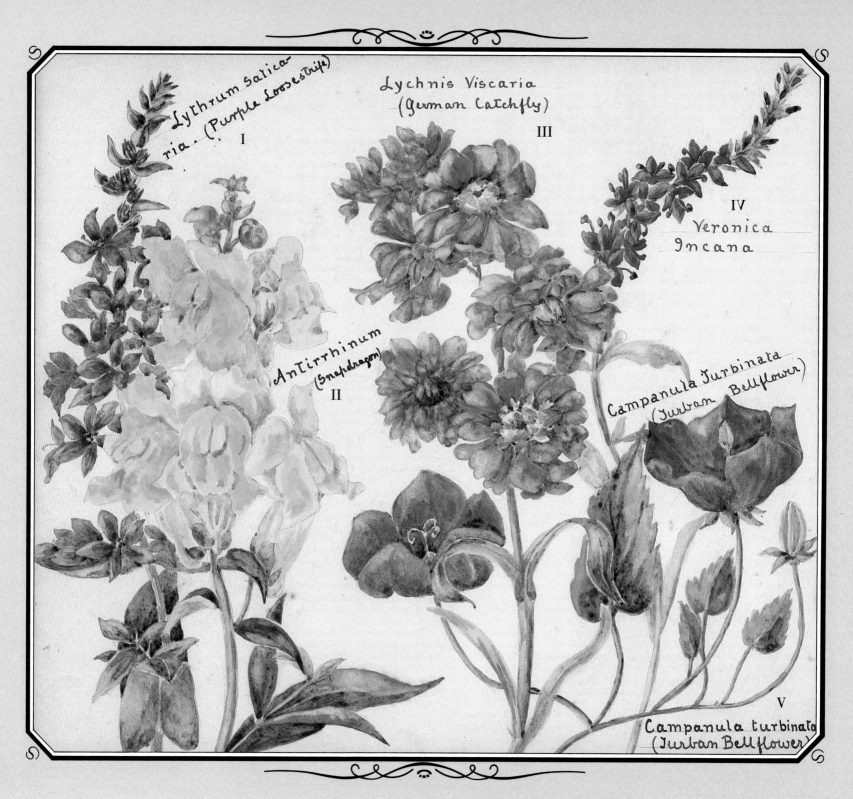

I *Lythrum salicaria* · Purple loosestrife II *Antirrhinum* sp. · Snapdragon
III *Lychnis viscaria* · German catchfly IV *Veronica incana*
V *Campanula turbinata* · Turban bellflower

Centauria Macrocephala
(Great golden Knapweed.)
II

Lysimachia clethroides
(Japanese Loosestrife)
III

Monarda didyma
(Oswega Tea or Bee Balm)
I

Gentiana septemfida
(Crested Gentian)
IV

I *Monarda didyma* · Bergamot   II *Centauria macrocephala* · Knapweed
III *Lysimachia clethroides* · Japanese loosestrife
IV *Gentiana septemfida* · Gentian

can be raised from seed, but the Victorian bedding calceolarias also included a range of other shrubby species such as *C. amplexicaulis* and hybrids that did not come true from seed. They were propagated by cuttings as half-hardy 'biennials' and pinched back to form bushy plants although they were always difficult and prone to die without warning, leaving beds of bare woody stalks at the height of summer. 'Sunshine' or similar cultivars would suffice but experiment with *C. amplexicaulis* and its relatives too if you can find them and have time and patience. Seed and plants. 45cm/18in (by cutting back).

Calendula officinalis
(Pot marigold)

CALENDULA Compositae
BEDDING **HA**

Marigold Unfortunately, the marigolds of the second half of the twentieth century tend to be F_1 hybrid African and French forms – *Tagetes erecta* and *T. patula*. These species were certainly grown in the nineteenth century, especially in the latter years, but were often talked of merely as substitutes for calendulas. I do not recommend them for the Victorian garden because the modern forms are so very different from the old types. but the old pot marigold, *C. officinalis*, is quite another matter. Of uncertain origin, it has been cultivated since the late sixteenth century and many of the variants have been known for many years. Choose a modern mixture but avoid the very large, very showy types and also the more recent compact selections such as 'Fiesta Gitana'. Some seed catalogues still list the old variety *prolifera*, known as the Hen and Chickens Marigold, in which the normal double flower is surrounded by secondary blooms. Seed. 60cm/2ft.

CALTHA Ranunculaceae
WATER GARDEN, DAMP BORDER **HP**

Marsh Marigold An invaluable spring-flowering native plant for any damp, poorly drained bed. The double flowered yellow form, now usually called 'Plena', was very popular although I share Gertrude Jekyll's preference for the single. The white Himalayan 'Alba' may be more recent for it was never mentioned in Victorian literature. Plants. 30cm/12in.

CAMASSIA Liliaceae
HERBACEOUS BORDER, WATER GARDEN **HP**

Quamash A good companion for its similarly blue-flowered relative, *Agapanthus*, although the flowers are borne in denser spikes. It also requires rather moister conditions. There are several species, including some with white flowers, all North American (the common name is that used by the Indians who ate the bulbs), but *C. quamash* is the best. Bulbs. 75cm/2ft 6in. PAGE 116.

CAMPANULA Campanulaceae
HERBACEOUS BORDER, ROCK GARDEN **HP**

Harebell, Bellflower A very large genus that includes some excellent rock garden species, but the border types were especially popular. There are many modern selections, but for authenticity choose true species or old garden forms of which several are readily available. For the rock garden, or front of border, the forms of *C. carpatica* (15-45cm/6-18in) offer an excellent range, while towards the centre or back of the border, the blue bells of *C. persicifolia* (100cm/3ft) are always welcome, although it is essential to stake them very early. Plants. PAGES 100, 128.

CARDAMINE Cruciferae
ROCK GARDEN **HA**

Lady's Smock, Bittercress Regrettably, most gardeners today know only *C. hirsuta*, the Hairy Bittercress, as one of the up and coming weeds of our time. Formerly, however, several European species of *Cardamine*, such as the little white-flowered alpine *C. trifolia*, also made useful additions to the cultivated flora. Seed. 15cm/6in. PAGE 132.

CENTAUREA Compositae
HERBACEOUS BORDER **HP**

Cornflower, Knapweed A large genus of over 600 species of plants with rather thistle-like flowers for a wide range of situations. One of the most popular for the back of the Victorian border or in the shrubbery and still freely available, although neglected, was the tall yellow *C. macrocephala*. *C. glastifolia* was a less common but otherwise similar species grown at Seggieden. Plants. 1-1.5m/3-5ft. PAGES 101, 104, 112.

CHAENOMELES Rosaceae
SHRUBBERY, WALLS **S (m)**

Ornamental Quince One of the most useful of the spring-flowering wall shrubs, related to the edible quince and once placed in the same genus, *Cydonia*, from which it differs in having toothed leaves. To add to the confusion, one of the common species, *C. speciosa*, which hails from China, was also once known as the Japan Apple Tree – and called *Pyrus japonica*, which means Japanese pear. But there are in fact three plants to consider: *C. japonica* from Japan (about 1m/3ft), introduced to Britain around 1869, *C. speciosa* (6m/20ft), introduced in 1796, and *C. × superba* (2m/6ft), a hybrid between the two. There are many cultivars of the latter two but some of the best are very recent and the most suitable choice would be 'Knap Hill Scarlet' (1870) and 'Cardinalis' (1885). Plants. PAGES 15, 132.

CHAMAEDAPHNE Ericaceae
SHRUBBERY **S (s)**

Chamaedaphne calyculata is one of several plants once called *Andromeda* but subsequently moved from that genus. It is a low-growing, rather pretty if wiry, white-flowered North American shrub for peaty soil. The dwarf variety *nana* is a better plant although of uncertain age. Plants. PAGE 97.

CHEIRANTHUS Cruciferae
HERBACEOUS BORDER, CONTAINERS **HB/HP**

Wallflower A long-time garden favourite although yet another plant for which the range of available cultivars has diminished rapidly in recent years in favour of motley mixtures. Ignore these and the dwarf 'Tom Thumb' types and choose some of the pure-coloured modern forms, although the real gems of the Victorian garden were the doubles that could be perpetuated only by cuttings. Almost all have gone, but you must have the old double yellow 'Harpur Crewe'. Seed or plants. 30-45cm/12-18in. PAGE 17.

CHELIDONIUM Papaveraceae
HERBACEOUS BORDER **HP**

Greater Celandine A native plant rarely seen in gardens today, other than as a weed, although it is freely available and useful, if unexciting. Seed. 30-60cm/1-2ft. PAGE 93.

CHELONE Scrophulariaceae
HERBACEOUS BORDER **HP**

Shellflowers How many gardeners today would know a shellflower if they tripped over it? Very few, yet these North American white- or reddish-flowered relatives of penstemons were once grown widely as middle of the border plants. You will no doubt find the name *Chelone* in many catalogues, although it is used for a plant better known as *Penstemon barbatus*, or alternatively for the medicinal herb, *C. glabra*. But the popular Victorian plant that I commend and that grew at Seggieden was *C. obliqua*, a 60cm/2ft tall species with a dense terminal spike of deep rose-pink flowers. It will need some searching for nonetheless. Seed. PAGE 124.

CHIONODOXA Liliaceae
ROCK GARDEN, FRONT OF BORDER, CONTAINER **HP**

Beautiful spring bulbs, usually with star-shaped blue or lilac-blue flowers; lovely growing through gravel. *C. luciliae* and its larger forms *gigantea* or *grandiflora* were and still are favourites. Bulbs. 15-20cm/6-8in. PAGES 97, 109.

CHRYSANTHEMUM Compositae
HERBACEOUS BORDER **HP**

Chrysanthemum-growing in Victorian times, as now, attracted a specialist gardening fraternity, spurred on by the species and forms sent home from the Far East by Robert Fortune and others. There is a large literature available for those interested in the detailed history of cultivars and techniques. For the more general gardener, however, a few points may be made. Until the second half of the nineteenth century when Japanese cultivars arrived in Western Europe, the most important types were of the Chinese tightly incurved form. Early flowering outdoor chrysanthemums did not appear in Britain until the end of the nineteenth century and the Koreans not until very recently. The old Chinese cultivars and the early Japanese introductions have all long gone and, given a choice of plants for the late Victorian border, preference should probably be given to a selection of modern pompons (or pompones as they were formerly known) as this type, derived from the Chinese Chusan Daisy collected by Robert Fortune in 1846, was especially popular in the nineteenth century. It

Chelone obliqua
(Turtle-head)

Chelone barbata

Centauria Glastifolia
Woad-leaved Centaury

I

Aster Amellus bessarabicus
Large Purple Aster

III

IV

II
Sedum Repens

I *Centauria glastifolia* · Centaury   **II** *Sedum repens*
III *Aster amellus* var. *bessarabicus* · Dwarf Michaelmas daisy   **IV** *Cyclamen* sp.

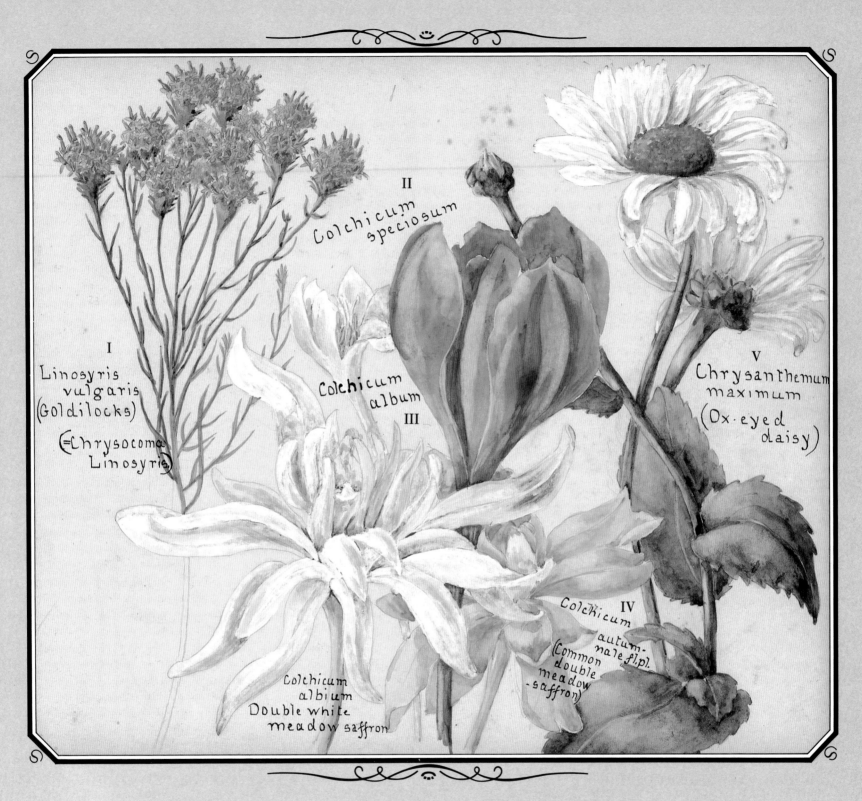

I *Linosyris vulgaris (Goldilocks) (=Chrysocoma Linosyris)*

II *Colchicum speciosum*

Colchicum album

III

IV *Colchicum autumnale fl.pl. (Common double meadow-saffron)*

Colchicum albium Double white meadow saffron

V *Chrysanthemum maximum (Ox-eyed daisy)*

I *Aster linosyris (= Linosyris vulgaris)* II *Colchicum speciosum*
III *Colchicum albicum* IV *Colchicum autumnale* V *Chrysanthemum maximum*

often surprises the modern gardener to read of the Victorians classifying chrysanthemums as wall plants, but the tall types were commonly used in this way or as screening.

Among other plants in the genus *Chrysanthemum*, mention must be made of a Victorian favourite, *C. maximum*, the Shasta Daisy (now more correctly placed in the genus *Leucanthemum*), although, like all chrysanthemums, it must be staked early to succeed. PAGE 105.

CINERARIA Compositae
BEDDING **HHA**

This plant has nothing to do with the florist's cineraria but is actually *Senecio cineraria*, the familiar half-hardy annual grown as bedding for its silvery white, deeply indented leaves which set off other bedding colours. 'Silverdust' is the most widely seen cultivar. Seed. 20cm/8in.

CLEMATIS Ranunculaceae
HERBACEOUS BORDER **HP**

Clematis are too well known to merit description but two important points should be made with respect to their use and selection. In the nineteenth century, they were grown at least as much as border perennials as climbers, being allowed to form a floriferous mound of growth with shoots pegged down at intervals during the summer. They can be very effective when grown in this way although you should not underestimate the area that will be needed. The few plants such as *C. integrifolia* and *C. recta* that we call herbaceous clematis and grow in this manner today were known then as dwarfs. Second, many of the present-day cultivars are of recent origin (although some old ones still survive) and certain popular species such as *C. tangutica* are post-Victorian introductions. Among particular Victorian favourites still readily obtainable are 'Beauty of

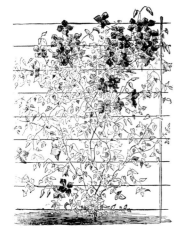

Clematis × jackmanii

Clematis viticella

Worcester', 'Belle of Woking', 'Duchess of Edinburgh', 'Gipsy Queen', 'Jackmannii', *C. viticella* and *C. lanuginosa* (a parent of many modern cultivars).

COLCHICUM Liliaceae
HERBACEOUS BORDER, ROCK GARDEN, GRASS **HP**

Meadow Saffron Bulbous autumn plants, a little like overgrown crocuses. Apart from the small rock garden forms, they really benefit from the physical and aesthetic support of tall grass. There are several so-called species, apparently merely varieties, but *C. autumnale*, in a range of colours and including the popular double form, would provide a good selection. Bulbs. 30cm/12in. PAGE 105.

COLEUS Labiatae
BEDDING **HHA**

Like so many other plants now grown only as pot or house plants, the coleus was formerly an important half-hardy bedding subject. Once there were several dozen cultivars of *C. blumei*, propagated by cuttings. These seem to have vanished, certainly from general catalogues, and we are left with mixtures and a few named cultivars to raise from seed. A popular Victorian cultivar was 'Vesuvius' and there is a modern one called 'Volcano' but they are not related. Seed. 30cm/12in.

Convallaria majalis (Lily-of-the-valley)

CONVALLARIA Liliaceae
SHADE **HP**

Lily-of-the-Valley A very old and popular plant, for which space must be found. But be warned, it is invasive and is best given a shady corner and left alone. Especially praised in the nineteenth century and still available, although neglected, are the double white 'Flore Pleno' and the stripe-leaved 'Variegata'. Rhizomes. 25cm/10in.

CORNUS Cornaceae
SHRUBBERY, SPECIMEN S (s-l)/T (s)

Dogwood The genus *Cornus* is a large one, generally restricted in gardens today to the variegated dog-woods and related forms planted for their winter bark colour. The principal species among these, *C. alba*, has been cultivated since the eighteenth century but the attractive cultivars are almost all recent. A better representative of the genus *Cornus* for the nineteenth-century garden would be *C. mas*, the Cornelian Cherry Tree, the mainstay of yellow-flowering winter trees before the Oriental witch hazels arrived after 1860. There is a lovely variegated form called 'Aurea Elegantissima' which is somewhat slower growing and dates from 1872. Plants. 14m/45ft. PAGE 109.

CORONILLA Leguminosae
ROCK GARDEN, FRONT OF BORDER **HP**

Crown Vetch *Coronilla varia* is another example of the Victorians' inventiveness. It is a southern European weed but provides very good close cover over low walls, adorning them with rich pink all summer through. Seed. 30cm/12in. PAGE 136.

CORYDALIS Papaveraceae
FRONT OF BORDER, SHADE, ROCK GARDEN, WALLS **HP**

Fumitory A huge genus of greatly neglected plants, including some out and out weeds but with some very useful species too. *C. bulbosa* (formerly called *C. cava*) is very useful for it bears its small bluish purple flowers and rather fern-like foliage in spring but then quickly disappears below ground to make way for grander plants. The yellow-flowered *C. lutea* was once very popular and spreads readily and prettily in partial shade. Although they can be grown as border plants, they are a little too invasive for comfort. Seed or plants. 15cm/6in. PAGES 77, 108.

COTONEASTER Rosaceae
SHRUBBERY, LOW WALLS, ROCK GARDEN S (s)

There are many species of these popular and extremely easily grown shrubs, some low and spreading, others tall and robust, but none easier and more useful today than *C. horizontalis* (1m/3ft). Although it was introduced to Britain from China as

recently as 1870, it soon proved itself tolerant of late nineteenth-century air pollution. *C. microphyllus* (1m/3ft), a rather similar species but evergreen, was much earlier while *C. simonsii* (4m/13ft), a mid-century arrival, was and is a useful hedging plant. Plants. PAGE 16.

CROCOSMIA Iridaceae
HERBACEOUS BORDER **HP**

Monbretia The familiar orange-flowered garden monbretia is a hybrid, *C. × crocosmiflora*, the result of a cross between the two South African species, *C. aurea* and *C. pottsii*, raised in France as late as 1880, but very rapidly becoming popular. It is an evocative plant of old gardens but is invasive and must be watched carefully. There are many modern cultivars but the original hybrid is still usually obtainable as seed. 1m/3ft. PAGE 125.

CROCUS Liliaceae
ALMOST ANYWHERE **HP**

The pity about crocuses is that so many gardeners grow only the large-flowered Dutch cultivars, some of which are nonetheless very old, at least in general form. Even in the Victorian period many others were available (one of the standard reference books on the genus was published in 1886). *C. sieberi*, *C. imperati* and *C. chrysanthus*, as grown at Seggieden, would be excellent starts, but *C. ancyrensis*, *C. laevigatus* and *C. tommasinianus* are among many others. Modern catalogues list improved forms of most species. Some are recent but some may be old, as considerable variation was also described in nineteenth-century listings. Corms. 10-20cm/4-8in. PAGES 16, 17, 77, 152.

CYCLAMEN Primulaceae
SHADE **HP**

Sowbread There are only two unfamiliar features of cyclamen today – the old name, sowbread, and their place in the primula family. A few of the marginally hardy species are recent introductions but the autumn-flowering *C. hederifolium* and the early spring-flowering *C. coum* have been part of British gardens for centuries. Corms. 10cm/4in. PAGE 104.

***Coleus blumei*
'Sutton's prize'**

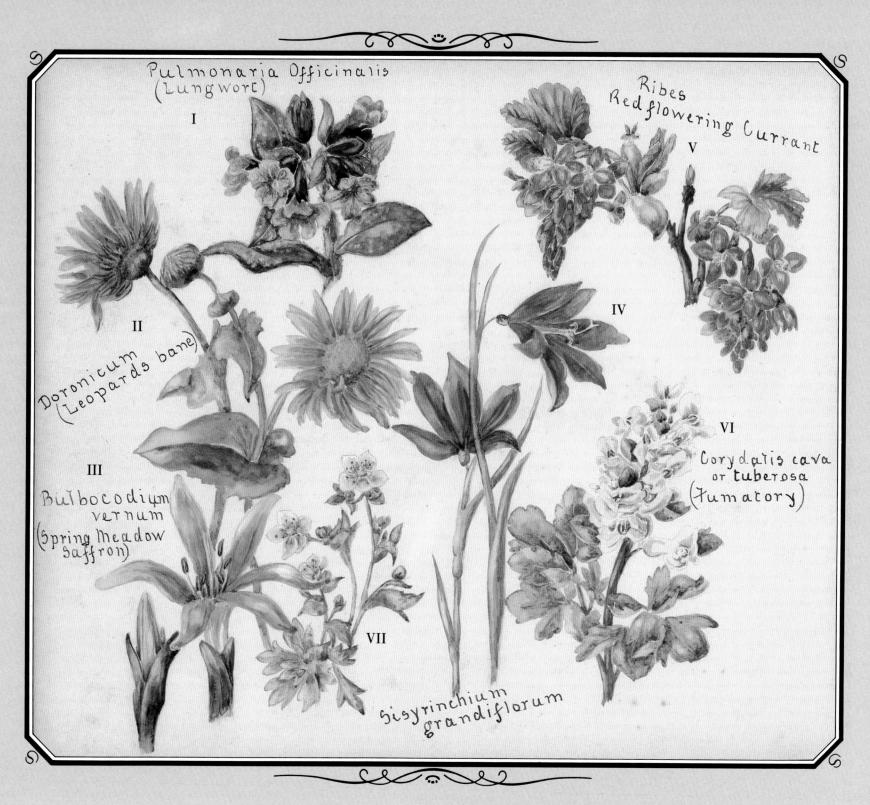

Pulmonaria Officinalis
(Lungwort)
I

Ribes
Red flowering Currant
V

Doronicum
(Leopards bane)
II

IV

III
Bulbocodium
vernum
(Spring Meadow
Saffron)

VI
Corydalis cava
or tuberosa
(Fumatory)

VII

Sisyrinchium
grandiflorum

I *Pulmonaria officinalis* · Lungwort   **II** *Doronicum* sp. · Leopard's bane
III *Bulbocodium vernum* · Spring meadow saffron
IV *Sisyrinchium grandiflorum*   **V** *Ribes* sp. · Flowering currant
VI *Corydalis bulbosa (= cava)* · Fumitory   **VII** *Veronica cinerea*(?)

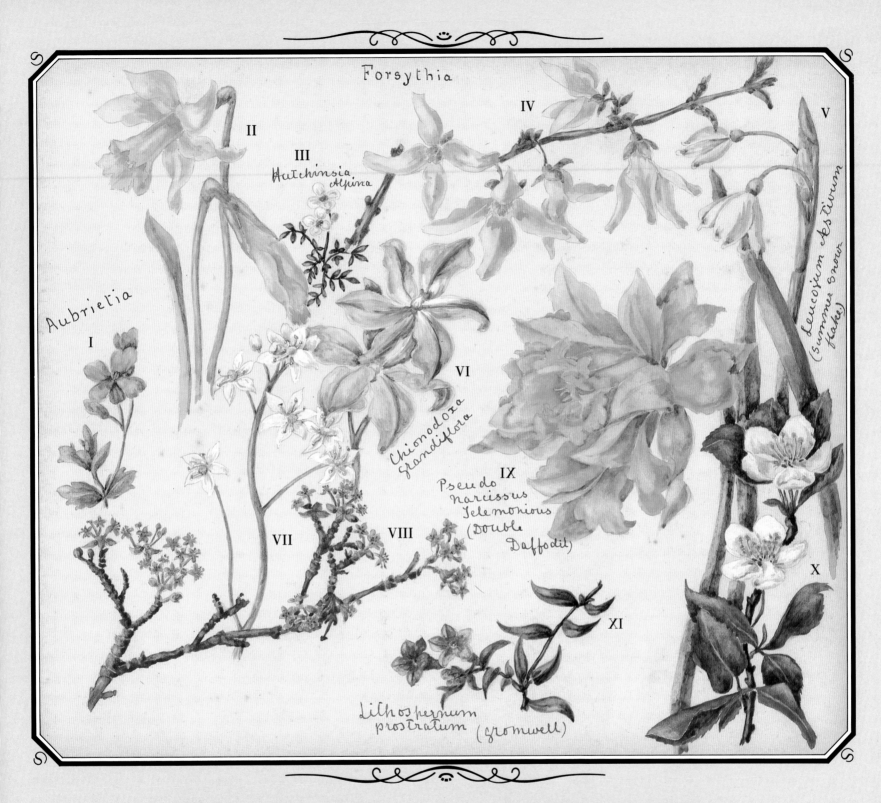

Forsythia

Aubrietia

Hutchinsia alpina

Chionodoxa grandiflora

Pseudo narcissus Telemonious (Double Daffodil)

Leucojum Aestivum (summer snow flake)

Lithospermum prostratum (gromwell)

I *Aubrieta* · Aubretia   II *Narcissus* sp. · Daffodil   III *Hutchinsia alpina*   IV *Forsythia* sp.

V *Leucojum aestivum* · Summer snowflake   VI *Chionodoxa luciliae (= grandiflora)* · Glory of the snow

VII *Scilla* or *Ornithogalum* sp.   VIII *Cornus mas*(?) · Cornelian cherry   IX *Narcissus* sp. · Double daffodil

X *Prunus cerasifera* 'Pissardii'(?) · Purple-leaved plum   XI *Lithospermum prostratum* · Gromwell

D

DABOECIA Ericaceae
PEAT GARDEN **S (d)**

St Dabeoc's Heath A native Irish plant for acid soils or the peat bed, cultivated since the early nineteenth century and with large, heath-like purple flowers from summer until well into the autumn. It was an unusual but inspired choice for Seggieden and worthy of a place with the more familiar heaths and heathers. The white form *alba* arose naturally and has been cultivated for almost as long as the type. Plants. 30-75cm/1ft-2ft 6in. PAGES 73, 93, 116.

DAHLIA Compositae
HERBACEOUS BORDER **HHP**

Florist's Dahlia

The dahlia divides gardeners almost as no other flower into those who love them and those who loathe them. The modern garden dahlia has its origins in several Mexican species, introduced to Britain from 1789 onwards. The cactus form, for instance, is derived from *D. juarezii* which did not arrive until 1864. Among the types that became especially popular during the nineteenth century were the Double Show and Fancy Dahlias, flowers of double, globular form rather similar to the modern Pompon but larger and looser headed. Plants derived from these became known later as Ball Dahlias. Some of the old types survive, but there is one dahlia that would be my

***Dahlia juarezii* (Cactus dahlia)**

choice to represent the genus. 'Bishop of Llandaff', although twentieth-century, looks much older and is one of the simplest yet loveliest dahlias ever raised, with deeply dissected red-purple foliage and single scarlet flowers. Plants. 1m/3ft.

DENTARIA Cruciferae
ROCK GARDEN, FRONT OF SHADY BORDER **HP**

Toothwort Named from their fang-like roots, the toothworts were once popular and useful plants for rather difficult sites but have virtually disappeared from catalogues. There are several species, related to *Cardamine* but with predominantly red flowers in spring. Plants or seed. 30cm/12in. PAGE 53.

DEUTZIA Hydrangeaceae
SHRUBBERY **S (m-l)**

This is a large shrub genus, sometimes placed in the saxifrage family and easily grown, but needing shelter from late frosts. *D. scabra* was a popular summer-flowering Victorian species from China and Japan with long, fairly upright clusters of white, rather bell-like flowers. The double form 'Plena', with a purple flush to the blooms, was especially prized. Plants. 3-3.5m/10-11ft. PAGE 76.

DIANTHUS Caryophyllaceae
BEDDING, FRONT OF SUNNY BORDER, ROCK GARDEN **HP/HB**

Pinks, Carnations The history of carnation growing is a subject enthusiasts will wish to pursue. There are also many exquisite rock garden species that have been cultivated. Nonetheless, the easiest to find of authentically old and historically interesting *Dianthus* cultivars are the exquisitely perfumed and delicately shaded old garden pinks such as 'Mrs Sinkins', 'Sam Barlow' and 'Inchmery' and the even older and lovelier laced pinks such as 'Dad's Favourite' and 'Paisley Gem'. (The 'Allwoodii' pinks are more recent.) But the same genus includes *D. barbatus*, the Sweet William, neglected today but so popular in former times that one Victorian writer remarked that praising it was like 'gilding refined gold'. The old cultivars have gone, so modern mixtures of both singles and doubles must substitute. Seed or plants. 30cm/12in. PAGE 116.

DICENTRA Fumariaceae
HERBACEOUS BORDER **HP**

Bleeding Heart A uniquely attractive perennial with long, graceful stems of rose-red and white flowers that has appealed to gardeners since it was first introduced to Britain from Japan in 1816. It needs shelter but is rather special. Plants. 45-75cm./1ft 6in-2ft 6in. PAGE 40.

DICTAMNUS Rutaceae
HERBACEOUS BORDER **HP**

Burning Bush Sometimes called by its old name of *Fraxinella* and an old garden favourite, with dense spikes of purple flowers and an aroma of lemon and balsam. On a hot summer day, the buildup of volatile oils above the flowers can be ignited, hence the common name. Seed or plants, 70cm/2ft 4in. PAGE 65.

DIGITALIS Scrophulariaceae
HERBACEOUS BORDER, SHADE GARDEN **HB/HP**

Foxglove No garden could be without foxgloves, which are often reliably perennial in many gardens, although biennial but perpetuating by self-seeding in others. There are modern selected forms, but a mixture of the original whites and purples would be better. Seed. PAGE 149

DODECATHEON Primulaceae
SHADE GARDEN **HP**

American Cowslip Delightful, reddish purple, cyclamen-like flowers for springtime. *D. maedia* is one of the longest cultivated and easiest to grow. Seed. 30-45cm/12-18in. PAGE 41.

DONDIA Umbelliferae
ROCK GARDEN, FRONT OF BORDER **HP**

Now usually called *Hacquetia epipactis*, this little clump-forming perennial has tight button-like yellow flowers surrounded by a green collar. It is an easy plant to grow and the only difficulty is to find a source of supply. Seed. 15-25cm/6-10in. PAGE 88.

DORONICUM Compositae
HERBACEOUS BORDER **HP**

Leopard's Bane Tall, yellow-flowered daisy-like plants, very popular in the Victorian border and very easy to grow, but plagued with mildew. There are modern selections with some disease resistance but the popular old species was *D. caucasicum*, still readily obtainable. Seed. 90cm/3ft. PAGE 108.

DRYAS Rosaceae
ROCK GARDEN **HP**

Mountain Avens Not especially characteristic of the Victorian garden but another inspiring little plant to find at Seggieden, not too far from its native mountain habitat (from which it might just have been lifted before legislation outlawed such practices). Small white flowers and toothed leaves with woolly undersides combine in a uniquely attractive manner. Seed. 10cm/4in. PAGE 41.

ECHEVERIA Crassulaceae
BEDDING **HHP**

This group, listed today only as 'house plants or greenhouse perennials', played a very important part in the intricate patterning of nineteenth-century carpet bedding when they tended to be grown as half-hardy biennials, seed being sown in one spring for planting out the next. Many different species of these fleshy American succulents were grown, each with particular foliage features. Specialist succulent nurseries still list vast numbers of different echeverias, including many recent hybrids, although these are intended for growing as individual specimens. For bedding, the best plan is probably to buy seed (much more cheaply than plants), of mixed species and to multiply individually appealing colour forms by offsets, cuttings or leaf cuttings. Seed.

ECHINOPS Compositae
HERBACEOUS BORDER **HP**

Globe Thistle Although forming large, rather coarse, spreading plants, the flowers are interesting and worth waiting for. The European species of globe

Doronicum caucasicum
(Leopard's bane)

I *Jasminum officinale* · Summer jasmine   **II** *Eryngium* sp. · Sea holly
III *Centaurea macrocephala* · Hardhead   **IV** *Veronica spicata*(?)
V *Colutea* × *media* · Bladder senna

I *Physostegia virginiana* · Obedient plant **II** *Sanguisorba canadensis*
III *Phuopsis stylosa* **IV** *Veronica longifolia*

thistle have been planted in gardens at least since the early nineteenth century. The species now called *E. ritro* was, and still is, the best and most popular for the centre of the border where their large, almost spherical blue flower heads arise in late summer. Plants. 1-1.5m/3-5ft. PAGE 60.

EPIMEDIUM Berberidaceae
GROUND COVER IN SHADE **HP**

Barrenwort The semi-evergreen epimediums have uniquely delicate and attractive foliage. The European *E. alpinum* has probably been in cultivation for the longest time but several other species were introduced during the early nineteenth century, and that generally called *E.* × *rubrum* has perhaps the most attractive foliage of all. Plants. 20cm/8in. PAGE 20.

ERANTHIS Ranunculaceae
GROUND COVER, FRONT OF HERBACEOUS BORDER **HP**

Winter Aconite What better sign of the arrival of spring than aconites, and especially the naturalised *E. hyemalis* which has been recognised as a valuable garden plant for centuries? Tuck them into corners where they will spread with happy abandon – but, like snowdrops, always transplant them when in leaf. Plants (if not, tubers). 10cm/4in. PAGE 7.

EREMURUS Liliaceae
HERBACEOUS BORDER **HP**

Foxtail Lily These magnificent rhizomatous plants have never grabbed gardeners' enthusiasm in the way that they should have done. Most of the best species arrived in Britain as the Victorian period closed and would be perfectly appropriate at the back of the herbaceous border. There are modern hybrids, but choose the species like *E. robustus* or *E. aitchisonii* if you can find authentic stock. Plants. Up to 3m/ 10ft.

ERICA Ericaceae
ROCK GARDEN, FRONT OF BORDER, PEAT GARDEN **S(d)**

Dwarf Shrub Heaths Much too well known to need describing, almost all of the hardy (and even some of the tender South African) species have been culti-

Eryngium alpinum

vated for a very long time. Particularly valuable is the lime-tolerant winter-flowering species, long called *E. carnea* but now given back its old name *E. herbacea*. There has been an explosion in the numbers of cultivars of heaths, and particularly of this species, in recent years. For real Victorian authenticity, it would be safest to grow true species only. Plants. Up to 1m/3ft. PAGES 17, 152.

ERIGERON Compositae
FRONT OF BORDER **HP**

Several species of *Erigeron*, related to the native Fleabane, were to be found in Victorian borders. *E. hyssopifolium*, once sometimes called *Galatella*, was a popular North American species; others are still available although the named cultivars listed under *Erigeron* in modern catalogues are recent. Seed. 30cm/12in.

ERYNGIUM Umbelliferae
HERBACEOUS BORDER **HP**

Sea Holly Unlike most other members of their family, eryngiums of many different species have been cultivated in gardens for several hundred years. The common native sand-dune species *E. maritimum* is attractive enough but cannot compare in size and form with certain exotic species. Some are not perennial, but try *E. giganteum* (1-1.5m/3-5ft) from the Caucasus. Plants. PAGES 32, 112.

ERYTHRONIUM Liliaceae
SHADE GARDEN **HP**

Dog's Tooth Violets Something of a rarity in the Victorian garden (and still something of a rarity today) although long recognized as singularly beautiful plants for deep, rich soil under trees. The common reddish purple-flowered *E. dens-canis*, with its charming spotted leaves, is the commonest (and least expensive – an important consideration for none of the corms are cheap). Recently available are hybrids of the American *E. revolutum* or *E. tuolumnense*, such as 'Pagoda'. Corms. 30cm/12in. PAGE 52.

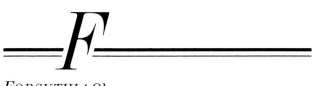

FORSYTHIA Oleaceae
SHRUBBERY **S (m)**

Indispensable for yellow blossom in late spring, but the choice of authentically old cultivars should be made with caution for there are many modern hybrids. Although the plant that is now called *F. × intermedia* (which in turn gave rise to such important modern cultivars as 'Lynwood' and 'Spectabilis'), originated in the late 1800s as a cross between *F. suspensa* and *F. viridissima*, it was not widely grown until the present century. A garden around 1890 would be more likely to have contained either the two parent Chinese species or the fine old form of *F. suspensa* called *fortunei*. Plants. 2-3m/6-10ft. PAGE 109.

FRITILLARIA Liliaceae
HERBACEOUS BORDER, GRASS **HP**

There are two very different common species of *Fritillaria*, the 1m/3ft tall Crown Imperial, *F. imperialis*, from western Asia, and the much smaller, nodding, native Snake's Head, *F. meleagris*. Both have long been popular garden plants, the Crown Imperial, despite its exotic origin, having been cultivated since the sixteenth century. Most of the various colour forms of Crown Imperial offered seem authentically old, although Victorian gardening books recommended a variegated leaved form that never seems to appear in catalogues today. Both species will be very much the better for being left in peace in the same site for several years. Bulbs. 1.5m/5ft. PAGES 21, 29, 117.

FUCHSIA Onagraceae
HERBACEOUS BORDER, BEDDING, CONTAINER **HP/HHP**

Unlike many other tender perennials, the non-hardy fuchsias never played a large part in Victorian bedding (less even than they do today) but they were very important as container plants on terraces and, as Hibberd put it, 'to form groups on the lawn on fête days'. There has been an explosion of cultivars in recent years but specialist nurseries still stock those old types that have stood the test of time. For containers, try the old cascading singles 'Autumnale' (scarlet and purple), 'Coachman' (pink and orange), or 'Mrs W. Rundle' (pink and orange), and the upright 'Countess of Aberdeen' (pink and white) or 'Lye's Unique' (white and orange-pink). For hardy cultivars, the choice is much greater and several dozen nineteenth-century forms are still with us. The best known of all, 'Mrs Popple', barely squeezes in, having been introduced in 1899, but the very popular 'display' (single pink) and the semi-double 'Mme Cornelisson' (red and white) are considerably older; and the earliest that I know of are the immensely endearing little single dwarf 'Tom Thumb' (red and mauve) and 'Query' (white, pink and violet) originating in 1850 and 1848 respectively. Plants. PAGES 54, 93.

GAILLARDIA Compositae
HERBACEOUS BORDER, BEDDING **HP/HHA**

Blanket Flowers The brightly coloured daisy-like North American gaillardias have never caught the gardening imagination in Britain to the extent they deserve, although the perennial *G. aristata* (about 75cm/2ft 6in) has been with us since the early nineteenth century and the annual *G. pulchella* even longer. Modern cultivars of both are available, but so are the original species. They make excellent cut flowers. Seed. PAGE 45.

GALANTHUS Liliaceae
FRONT OF BORDER, GRASS, SHADE, WOODLAND GARDEN **HP**

Snowdrop Who could contemplate spring without the snowdrop? It grows in wild or naturalized state throughout Europe and has been an essential part of British gardens for centuries. The common species is *G. nivalis* but this occurs in many forms, including the double 'Flore Pleno'; most are very old. The rather taller and more eastern species *G. elwesii* was introduced in 1875 and was grown at Seggieden; but most of the other species likely to be offered today were not introduced until the last decade of the nineteenth century. Bulbs (but best planted while still in growth). 8-30cm/3-12in. PAGES 7, 88, 89.

***Galanthus nivalis*
(Snowdrops)**

May

III

IV

VII

II

VIII

Primula
Auricula
(Common
Auricula)

I

V

Vinca
(Periwinkle)
VI

IX

Primula nivalis
(White villous
Auricula)

I *Primula auricula* · Auricula   **II** *Camassia scilloides*   **III** *Dianthus* sp. · Pink   **IV** *Narcissus* sp. · Narcissus
V *Phyllothamnus erectus*   **VI** *Vinca* sp. · Periwinkle   **VII** *Amelanchier* sp. · June berry
VIII *Daboecia cantabrica* · St Dabeoc's heath   **IX** *Primula* sp.

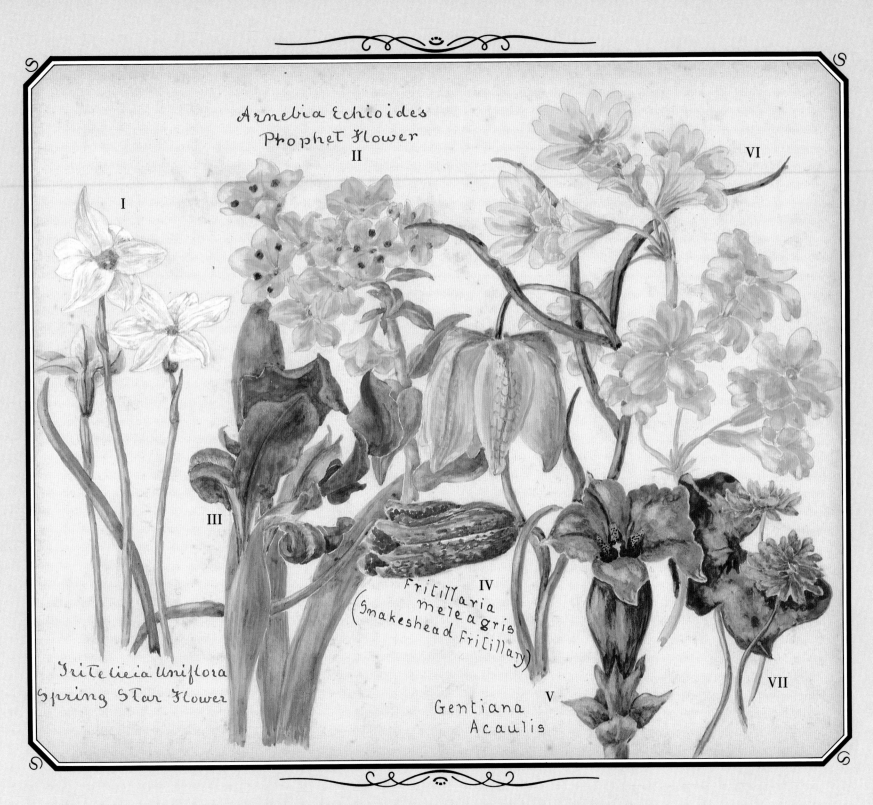

Arnebia Echioides
Prophet Flower
II

I

VI

III

IV
Fritillaria
meleagris
(Snakeshead Fritillary)

Triteleia Uniflora
Spring Star Flower

Gentiana
Acaulis
V

VII

I *Ipheion (= Trileleia) uniflora*   **II** *Arnebia echioides* · Prophet flower
III *Iris* sp.   **IV** *Fritillaria meleagris* · Snake's head fritillary
V *Gentiana acaulis* · Stemless gentian
VI *Paradisea liliastrum* · St Bruno's lily   **VII** *Hepatica triloba* 'Flore Pleno'

GALEGA Leguminosae
HERBACEOUS BORDER **HP**

Goat's Rue Yet another genus of once popular but now neglected hardy perennials. Related, interestingly, to *Wisteria*, they have deeply divided leaves and clusters of lilac or white pea-like flowers. *G. officinalis*, introduced to Britain as long ago as the sixteenth century, is freely available. Seed. 1-1.2m/3-4ft. PAGE 33.

GALTONIA Liliaceae
HERBACEOUS BORDER **HP**

Cape Hyacinth The South African galtonias are large plants with small, drooping, bell-like flowers and offer excellent late summer appeal. *G. candicans* is the commonest and longest cultivated species. Bulbs. 1-1.2m/3-4ft. PAGE 136.

GARRYA Garryaceae
SHRUBBERY, WALLS **S (l)**

The green catkins of *Garrya elliptica* do not necessarily offer the best way of brightening the gloom of midwinter, but it is a hardy enough evergreen shrub, widely planted since its introduction from western North America in 1828. The form called 'James Roof', with abnormally long catkins, is recent. Plants. PAGE 16.

GAULTHERIA Ericaceae
SHRUBBERY, GROUND COVER **S (m)**

Although *Gaultheria* is a fairly large genus of evergreens related to *Vaccinium*, only one species, the North American *G. shallon*, the Partridge Berry, is seen frequently. It was introduced to Britain early in the nineteenth century and its dense shrubby growth quickly gained favour on estates as game cover. Plants. 1.5m/5ft. PAGE 25.

GENTIANA Gentianaceae
FRONT OF BORDER, ROCK GARDEN, PEAT GARDEN **HP**

The gentians make up a huge genus of indispensable and utterly beautiful alpines. Many are difficult to grow and for specialists only, although the late summer-flowering *G. septemfida* (15-30cm/6-12in) from western Asia revels in peaty soils and is perhaps the easiest. The traditional English garden gentian is the sun-loving *G. acaulis* (5-10cm/2-4in). Give it a soil that is 'deep, firm, moist, stony, but is neither clay nor sand' was the advice offered in 1867. Plants. PAGES 77, 101, 117.

GERANIUM Geraniaceae
HERBACEOUS BORDER **HP**

Cranesbills Still unfortunately confused in many gardeners' minds with their half-hardy South African relatives, the pelargoniums, hardy geraniums are wonderfully varied, rewarding and evocative plants for any garden. Numerous cultivars have been bred and selected in recent years and many more species have become popular; but in the nineteenth century, the native bluish purple *G. pratense* (75-120cm/2ft 6in-4ft) and the lower-growing, bushy, red *G. sanguineum* almost always headed the lists. The flesh pink-flowered form of *sanguineum* called *lancastriense* is an old plant and was often recommended by Victorian gardeners. Plants.

Geranium sp.

GEUM Rosaceae
HERBACEOUS BORDER **HP**

There are some delightful dwarf geums for the rock garden, but the border species, which remind some gardeners of undernourished Japanese anemones, are fine plants and have seen a comeback in recent years, with several new cultivars on offer. There is, however, one gorgeous old one, as popular in the nineteenth century as it is today – 'Mrs J. Bradshaw' (60cm/2ft) is a fine double red form of *G. chiloense* and still readily available. Plants. PAGE 29.

GLADIOLUS Iridaceae
HERBACEOUS BORDER **HHP**

The history of the large-flowered garden gladiolus stretches back a long way. Many of the basic crosses were made during the Victorian period and by the end of the nineteenth century a wide range of types and

Gladiolus × *colvillei*

cultivars of a plant now usually called *G.* × *hortulanus* was available. They were grown as border plants and also in the kitchen garden for use as cut flowers – still an excellent plan if you don't wish to deplete the garden display. Most if not all of the old cultivars have succumbed to virus over the years; but well worth a place, too, in the Victorian garden was a smaller plant (about 45cm/18in) that was one of the first hybrids, dating from 1823. Generally called *G.* × *colvillei*, it is still frequently offered, usually as 'The Bride', and is hardy in many areas. Corms.

GYPSOPHILA Caryophyllaceae
HERBACEOUS BORDER **HP**

Traditionally popular for bouquets, the feathery sprays of white gypsophila flowers appear equally attractive when growing in the border. The species *G. paniculata* is still obtainable, although the most popular form today is 'Bristol Fairy', a twentieth-century cultivar, rather earlier flowering and stronger growing than the old double 'Flore Pleno'. Seed or plants. 1.5m/5ft. PAGE 149.

HAMAMELIS Hamamelidaceae
SHRUBBERY **S (l)/T (s)**

Witch Hazel Perhaps the queen of winter-flowering shrubs; there are few more stirring sights in the depths of January than the bare branches of the witch hazel as they spring to sparkling yellow life. The species seen most frequently in catalogues and gardens today is *H. mollis*, which Charles Maries brought back from China in 1879 (the fine form called 'Pallida' is more recent); but before this became widely available, the Japanese *H. japonica* was commonly seen, especially as the tall-growing cultivar 'Arborea'. Plants. 5m/16ft. PAGE 7.

HELENIUM Compositae
HERBACEOUS BORDER **HP**

Sneeze-weed Despite a name that might put off hay-fever sufferers, these are quite beautiful and easily grown North American perennials for the autumn

border. Those most commonly offered are forms of *H. autumnale* and were usually described in Victorian books under such names as *rubrum* or *superbum*, with a form called *pumillum* that was generally lower growing (about 30-60cm/1-2ft). It is difficult to determine which of the cultivars currently on offer equate with the old forms, although the very tall (up to 1.5m/5ft) 'Riverton Gem' is certainly an imposing and genuinely old gold and crimson-flowered plant. Plants. PAGE 128.

HELIANTHUS Compositae
HERBACEOUS BORDER **HHA/HP**

Sunflower The gigantic North American annual sunflower, *H. annuus*, has been a feature of British gardens since the sixteenth century. You should grow the basic species, however, for some of the forms now offered, especially those with some red coloration, are twentieth-century hybrids. Less commonly seen today is the once popular lower-growing (1-2m/3-6ft) perennial *H. decapetalus*, in its cultivated form *multiflorus*, which includes the double 'Flore Pleno'. Seed. PAGE 125.

HELIOTROPIUM Boraginaceae
BEDDING **HHA**

Heliotrope, Cherry Pie Unusual among bedding plants in being grown primarily for perfume rather than flower or foliage characteristics. It also shares with cinerarias and a few others the curious attribute of being a shrub grown as a half-hardy bedding annual. In the nineteenth century, many cultivars of *H. peruvianum* (now usually called *H. arborescens*) and *H. corymbosum* were available. You will be extremely fortunate to find them today, and indeed fortunate to find any named form other than the deep purple-flowered 'Marine'. Seed. 60cm/2ft (by cutting back).

HELLEBORUS Ranunculaceae
HERBACEOUS BORDER **HP**

The hellebores have retained their old popularity and are so valuable for their long flowering period and for their attractive, persistent foliage. You should certainly have the white-flowered Christmas Rose *H. niger*, dating back to the sixteenth century. The true

Gypsophila paniculata

Heliotropium peruvianum
(Cherry pie)

Schizostylis coccinea

I

III

II
Aster longifolius
(Rosy Starwort)

IV

I *Leucanthemum vulgare* · Ox-eye daisy
II *Aster longifolius* · Starwort, Michaelmas daisy   III *Schizostylis coccinea*
IV *Aster* sp. · Starwort, Michaelmas daisy

Lilium sp. · Lily

identity of many other species is shrouded by confusing hybrids, but *H. olympicus* was greatly admired in the nineteenth century. The presence of the much less common *H. abchasicus* and *H. purpurascens* at Seggieden indicated a special fondness for this genus. Plants. 45cm/18in. PAGES 7, 16, 17.

HEMEROCALLIS Liliaceae
HERBACEOUS BORDER HP

Day Lily Yet another genus that modern plant breeders have rediscovered and coaxed into a wide range of cultivars and colours. The individual flowers last for the proverbial day but the plant as a whole blooms for weeks. Fortunately, the old species and some of the old forms are still with us. Choose *H. fulva* and its double forms 'Flore Pleno' or 'Kwanso'. Plants. 30-90cm/1-3ft. PAGES 60, 64.

HEPATICA Ranunculaceae
ROCK GARDEN, SHADE HP

Liver Leaf An unattractive but descriptive name for a lovely little rock garden plant, related to anemones, and over which Victorian gardening writers waxed lyrical indeed. *H. triloba* (now usually called *H. nobilis*) was the most widely grown species. It is naturally very variable and existed in a large range of cultivars and colour forms. Plants or seed. 15cm/6in.

HEUCHERA Saxifragaceae
FRONT OF BORDER HP

Alum Root Useful for ground-covering foliage at the edge of borders but not exactly dramatic. The wild North American species *H. sanguinea* was introduced to Britain fairly late in the nineteenth century and acquired a reputation for being short-lived although some of its hybrid cultivars were more reliable. Probably some of the named forms offered today are old, although 'Bressingham' is certainly not. Plants or seed. 30-45cm/12-18in. PAGE 44.

HOSTA Liliaceae
HERBACEOUS BORDER, SHADE GARDEN, WATER GARDEN HP

Plantain Lily Generally known to the Victorians as funkias, the Oriental hostas were usually referred to in nineteenth-century books as if they were all

Iberis umbellata
(Annual candytuft)

Hosta sieboldiana

true species, although even then there existed a large range of hybrids of doubtful authenticity. Today, there are many dozens of cultivars, most emanating from North American nurseries. Perhaps the group is best represented by *H. sielboldiana* and *H. plantaginea* 'Grandiflora', which are still obtainable as plants seemingly the same as those the Victorians grew. Plants. 40-70cm/16-28in.

HUTCHINSIA Cruciferae
ROCK GARDEN, FRONT OF HERBACEOUS BORDER HP

Hutchinsia alpina is one of a group of small mat-forming white-flowered cruciferous plants that make useful additions either to the rock garden or small corners in the border. It has been cultivated at least since the second half of the eighteenth century and is still freely available. Seed. 8cm/3in. PAGE 109.

HYACINTHUS Liliaceae
HERBACEOUS BORDER, CONTAINERS HP

The familiar garden and pot hyacinths are derived from the Eastern Mediterranean species *H. orientalis* which has been cultivated for centuries. Some of the modern Dutch cultivars have a robustness of flower that bears little resemblance to the wild species or the older cultivated types which have vanished. Nonetheless, even these modern plants, when allowed to establish in the garden, very soon lose their sculptured perfection and would not be out of place in a Victorian setting. Bulbs. 30cm/12in. PAGE 53.

HYDRANGEA Hydrangeaceae
SHRUBBERY S (m-l)

Hydrangea today is synonymous with the blue or pink mop-headed forms of *H. macrophylla*, a poor image of a fine genus of which the finest representative of all, *H. paniculata grandiflora* (4-6m/13-20ft), grew at Seggieden. Most other *Hydrangea* species were in cultivation by the late nineteenth century and the delicate *H. aspera* (2-3m/6-10ft) should be included in any other than the most exposed gardens. Plants. PAGE 72.

IBERIS Cruciferae
FRONT OF HERBACEOUS BORDER, ROCK GARDEN **HA/HP**

Candytuft There are both annual and perennial candytufts, the former derived from *I. amara*. The wild form is readily obtained and is preferable to the newer cultivar mixtures. Perhaps the most popular perennial is the woody *I. gibraltarica*, also freely available. Seed. 8-30cm/3-12in.

ILEX Aquifoliaceae
SHRUBBERY **S (d)/T (m)**

Holly There are numerous species of holly, most having been cultivated for many years but most still uncommon. A representative group for the Victorian garden could include forms of *I. aquifolium* such as the Hedgehog Holly, 'Ferox', the yellow-edged 'Laurifolia Aurea' and the yellow-berried 'Bacciflava' with the best of the golden variegated cultivars of *I. × altaclarensis* called 'Golden King'. Plants. 15m/50ft. PAGE 15.

INULA Compositae
HERBACEOUS BORDER **HP**

Several species of *Inula*, a close relative of *Helenium*, have found their way into gardens but the one most characteristic of the old English garden is *I. helenium*, Elecampane, a tall, bright yellow-flowered medicinal herb. Seed is still readily obtained. 1.5m/5ft. PAGE 124.

IRESINE Amaranthaceae
BEDDING **HHP**

Bloodleaf Like *Coleus*, iresines today are thought of almost exclusively as house plants. However, they were once invaluable in bedding schemes for their attractive dark foliage and created something of a stir when first introduced in the second half of the nineteenth century. *I. herbstii* is the species usually offered as a pot plant, although *I. lindenii* was preferred for bedding. Seed or plants. 30cm/12in.

IRIS Iridaceae
HERBACEOUS BORDER, ROCK GARDEN **HP**

The many different groups and species of irises are among the most confusing of garden plants, although their flower form is distinctive enough to place them easily in their genus. There was very much less diversity in Victorian irises than there is today and although the nineteenth-century cultivars have almost certainly vanished, clumps of blue-flowered, tall-bearded irises among the other border plants would perhaps be the most appropriate representatives of the period, for the dwarf and intermediate bearded types are largely twentieth-century plants. Forms of the bulbous English and Spanish irises were important and popular too, as were some of the small rock garden species. Rhizomes and bulbs. 10cm-1m/4in-3ft. PAGES 44, 117.

JASMINUM Oleaceae
SHRUBBERY **S (m-l)**

Jasmine We commonly grow two species of jasmine today: the very hardy, yellow, winter-flowering *J. nudiflorum* (4m/3ft), and the more tender and beautifully fragrant white, summer-flowering *J. officinale* (3m/10ft). The former was one of Robert Fortune's introductions from China, arriving in Britain in 1844 and very soon becoming popular – as at Seggieden. The summer jasmine is a very much older and quite gloriously indispensable garden plant, probably too tender for Seggieden although a less common and interesting species also grown there was *J. humile wallichianum* (3m/10ft), sometimes incorrectly called *J. pubigerum*, which has the attributes of yellow flowers in summer and considerable hardiness. Plants. PAGES 15, 112, 145.

Iresine herbstii
'Aureo-reticulata'

Chelone Obliqua
(Turtle-Head)

I

III

II

Lychnis
chalcedonica
(Scarlet
Campion)

IV

Galatella hyssopifolia
(Hyssop-leaved
galatella)

V

latifolius albus Lathyrus
(White
Everlasting Pea)

I *Chelone obliqua*   **II** *Lychnis chalcedonica* · Campion   **III** *Inula* sp.
IV *Aster (= Galatella)* sp.   **V** *Lathyrus latifolius* · Everlasting pea

Montbretia crocosmæflora

I

II

III

Helianthus multiflorus. pl. (Sunflower)

Anemone japonica (Japan Anemone)

I *Crocosmia (= Montbretia) crocosmiflora* **II** *Helianthus annuus* · Sunflower
III *Anemone japonica* · Japanese anemone

Lathyrus grandiflorus
(Everlasting pea)

Lathyrus latifolius
(Everlasting pea)

KALMIA Ericaceae
SHRUBBERY **S (s-m)**

Less well known than their cousins, the rhododendrons, the North American kalmias are yet further examples of the glory of the heath family. 'Deep gritty peat, sun, clean air and exposure' was a Victorian recommendation for their successful cultivation, although they are not particularly easy plants to satisfy. The species seen most commonly is *K. latifolia*, sometimes called the Calico Bush or Mountain Laurel, introduced to Britain in the early eighteenth century. Choose the true species and avoid the modern hybrid cultivars. Plants. 4m/13ft. PAGE 25.

KERRIA Rosaceae
SHRUBBERY **S (s-m)**

Jew's Mallow I do not know how the common name of this plant originated but it has certainly been a feature of British gardens since the double form was introduced from Japan in 1804. It had long been a garden plant there (although in fact it is native to China) but not until the single type followed thirty years later did botanists appreciate the flower structure and realize that it was a member of the rose family. Plants. 2m/6ft. PAGES 28, 85.

KNIPHOFIA Liliaceae
HERBACEOUS BORDER **HP**

Red Hot Poker Although I have called them hardy perennials, most of these large African members of the lily family, once more commonly called torch lilies, are not reliably durable in most British gardens. The plant grown at Seggieden was *K. uvaria*, one of the hardiest, commonest and also one of the longest in cultivation, having been introduced as early as 1707. It has been used as the parent of many hybrids and unfortunately it is these modern hybrids that are most likely to be seen today, although specialist nurseries may have authentic species; *K. northiae* is one that is obtainable. Plants. 1m/3ft. PAGE 129.

Kniphofia caulescens

L

LANTANA Verbenaceae
BEDDING **HHA**

Lantanas are shrubs with small flowers massed into flattish heads of mixed colours, commonly seen along Mediterranean seafronts. But they were yet another example of a tender plant that the Victorians literally cut down to size and used for bedding. They were usually propagated from cuttings in spring, A considerable range of cultivars was once used (the evocatively named 'Impératrice Eugénie' was the most popular) but all that you are likely to find in general catalogues today is seed of 'Mixed Hybrids'. Specialist nurseries may still maintain a few named forms. Plants. 60cm/2ft (by cutting back).

LATHYRUS Leguminosae
HERBACEOUS BORDER **HP**

Ornamental Peas Every modern gardener is familiar with sweet peas, but the plant has come a long way from the forms that the Victorians knew. The ancestor of the modern sweet pea is *L. odoratus*, a native of the Mediterranean cultivated in Britain since about 1700, although a very limited range of colour forms was available until the very end of the Victorian period. The only extant pre-Victorian cultivar of which I am aware is 'Painted Lady'; modern sweet peas bear little resemblance to old types. Indeed, more typically Victorian would be the two related pea species grown at Seggieden – *L. grandiflorus* and the perennial that is appropriately called the Everlasting Pea, *L. latifolius*. It is propagated by cuttings and seemingly lasts forever. Both are readily available. Seed. 4m/13ft. PAGES 45, 124.

LEUCANTHEMUM Compositae
HERBACEOUS BORDER **HP**

The name *Leucanthemum* may be rather unfamiliar but several common daisy-like garden plants have found a home here. The Shasta Daisy, which I describe under its more familiar generic name *Chrysanthemum*, is one; but another refugee from the same genus is *L. vulgare*, the Ox-eye Daisy. This is sometimes also called Marguerite, a confusing name, better applied to the shrubby half-hardy perennial *L. frutescens*. The ox-eye daisy, a familiar although diminished wild plant in Britain, has been grown in gardens for centuries. Seed is readily obtainable. 60cm/2ft. PAGE 120.

LEUCOJUM Amaryllidaceae
HERBACEOUS BORDER **HP**

Snowflakes The two common species are *L. vernum* and *L. aestivum*, flowering in spring and summer respectively, and understandably often mistaken for out-of-season snowdrops, to which they are related. Both have been cultivated for centuries and although widely grown in the nineteenth century have inexplicably never approached the snowdrop in popularity. Bulbs. 20cm/8in. PAGES 88, 109.

LEYCESTERIA Caprifoliaceae
SHRUBBERY **S (s-m)**

The only species grown widely in nineteenth-century gardens was the plant most frequently seen today, *L. formosa*, a fairly hardy, deciduous Himalayan plant with purplish bell-like flowers, introduced in 1824. In Britain the fruits are greatly appreciated by pheasants and it is sometimes planted as game cover. Plants. 2m/6ft. PAGE 72.

LIATRIS Compositae
HERBACEOUS BORDER **HP**

Snakeroot Several species of these rather stately North American perennials were introduced to British gardens in the eighteenth century although the most widely grown was that seen at Seggieden, *L. spicata*, about 1m/3ft tall, with dense flower spikes of deep purple. True species may be unobtainable now but there are some modern compact cultivars that would suffice. Plants. PAGE 32.

LILIUM Liliaceae
HERBACEOUS BORDER, CONTAINERS **HP**

Lily Can an 'English garden' of whatever age be considered complete without lilies? In recent years, the explosion of reliable North American disease-resistant hybrids has brought lily growing within everyone's reach. In Victorian times, however, the range of cultivars was limited and many of the species succumbed to viruses. Two plants that were first introduced around 1600, *L. chalcedonicum* and the early-flowering Yellow Turk's Cap, *L. pyrenaicum*, among others, grew at Seggieden. But forced to choose the indispensable lily for a Victorian garden, I would opt for *L. candidum*, the white Madonna Lily (although you will need a modern fungicide to keep it free from *Botrytis*). Unfortunately, *L. regale*, arguably the finest of all lilies, was not sent back from China by Wilson until 1903, and is therefore not strictly correct for a Victorian garden. Bulbs. 2m/6ft. PAGES 61, 63, 65, 121.

LIMONIUM Plumbaginaceae
HERBACEOUS BORDER **HP**

Statice Although known to botanists as the Sea Lavenders (a group of bewildering complexity), the limoniums are most familiar to gardeners and flower arrangers as statice. Many species have been cultivated since the seventeenth century and *L. latifolium*, grown at Seggieden, is typical in its shrubby habit and tiny blue flowers in compact branched spikes. Modern cultivars exist but true species are also obtainable. Seed. 30cm/12in. PAGE 61.

LINDELOFIA Boraginaceae
HERBACEOUS BORDER **HP**

The Himalayan *Lindelofia longiflora* or, as it was once known, *L.* (or *Cynoglossum*) *spectabilis*, is typical of its family – a rather coarsely hairy plant, reminiscent of borage and hound's tongue, with bright blue, tubular flowers. It is not the most attractive plant in the world but is worthy of inclusion as a none too large or aggressive representative of a family once much more popular than today. Seed may still be obtainable. 45cm/18in. PAGE 64.

LITHOSPERMUM Boraginaceae
ROCK GARDEN **HP**

The 'modern' *Lithospermum* is *L. diffusum*, a prostrate rock plant with electric blue flowers, actually cultivated in Britain since 1825 but most familiar in the more recent form 'Heavenly Blue'. In the Vic-

Lillium candidum
(Madonna lily)

Lillium chalcedonicum
(Scarlet martagon)

I *Helenium autumnale* · Sneezewort   II *Lonicera* sp. · Honeysuckle
III *Campanula persicifolia*

Tritoma Uvaria, or
Kniphofia Uvaria
Common Flame Flower
I

II

III

I *Kniphofia uvaria* · Flame flower, Red hot poker   **II** *Aster amellus*
III *Aster (cordifolius?)*

**Lobelia cardinalis
(Cardinal flower)**

Lobelia fulgens

Lobelia syphilitica

torian garden, a related and more important species was *L. fruticosum*, a more upright plant, tolerant of lime, which *L. diffusum* is not. Seed or plants. 30cm/12in. PAGE 109.

LOBELIA Campanulaceae
HERBACEOUS BORDER, BEDDING **HHA/HP**

Lobelias need no introduction to the modern gardener who grows, as half-hardy bedding annuals, cultivars such as 'Crystal Palace', derived from the perennial South African *L. erinus*. The species was introduced to Britain in 1752 and played an important part in Victorian bedding, but as with so many plants now grown from seed, the nineteenth-century gardener relied heavily on the propagation of named lobelia cultivars such as 'Brighton', 'Swanley Blue', 'Trentham Blue' and 'Annie' by cuttings. These were taken towards the end of summer from plants specially cut back to produce a proliferation of suitable shoots. Such forms have all disappeared and there is no alternative today but to use modern named hybrids; but you are advised to avoid mixtures. Seed. 10-15cm/4-6in.

Also important in the Victorian garden were the taller, hardier herbaceous lobelias derived from the North American red-flowered *L. cardinalis* and *L. fulgens*, and the blue-flowered *L. syphilitica*. They require winter protection in colder areas and need moist conditions everywhere; indeed they are often sold today as water or bog garden plants. Very few of the old forms are still available but the true species and 'Victoria' (often called 'Queen Victoria'), a form of *L. fulgens*, are still with us – the latter has not only rich scarlet flowers but also beetroot-red leaves. Seed or plants. 90cm/3ft.

LONICERA Caprifoliaceae
SHRUBBERY, WALLS **S (s)/Climber**

Honeysuckle One of the small number of plants that most gardeners would name as essential in an English garden of whatever age. The commonest of the rather untidy climbing forms is the deciduous *L. periclymenum*, a native species once known more generally as Woodbine. Some cultivars of this plant have been grown in Britain since the seventeenth century; 'Belgica', the so-called Early Dutch Honeysuckle, with early summer flowers coloured red-purple on

the outside, is probably the oldest, but 'Serotina', the late summer-flowering Late Red or Dutch, is almost as old. Almost all other loniceras seen today are more recent introductions, although the evergreen *L. japonica* (including its distinctly variegated cultivar 'Aureo-reticulata') was a nineteenth-century arrival. Although several shrubby species were introduced in the Victorian period, especially from Asia, the shrubby type most frequently seen today, *L. nitida*, was not introduced by Wilson until 1908. The common sprawling shrub called *L. × heckrottii*, an American cross between *L. sempervirens* and *L. americana*, seems to have originated at the end of the nineteenth century but was not grown widely until the twentieth. Plants. 6m/20ft (climbers). PAGE 128.

LUNARIA Cruciferae
HERBACEOUS BORDER **HA/HB**

Honesty *Lunaria annua* (sometimes called *L. biennis*) is a European species cultivated in Britain since 1595 and too well known to need describing. It often occurs in naturalized state as an escape from cultivation. Its greatest merit is not its flowers but the flat, silvery seed heads which are so useful for dried flower arrangements. The deep purple-flowered 'Munstead Purple' is presumably the plant that Gertrude Jekyll called 'dark honesty' and would be an appropriate choice. Seed. 1m/3ft. PAGE 29.

LUPINUS Leguminosae
HERBACEOUS BORDER **HP**

Lupin Another of the indispensables for a herbaceous border, but be especially wary when selecting cultivars. Most of the lupins offered in catalogues today (such as the Russell hybrids) are twentieth-century plants, strikingly different from Victorian forms. These modern types are derived from the North American *L. polyphyllus* (introduced to Britain in 1826), often through crosses with the larger, shrubby *L. arboreus*. *L. polyphyllus* itself was grown at Seggieden (together with the interesting dwarf species *L. lepidus*) and as seed of this plant is still freely obtainable, it might be the best choice as a contrast to modern hybrids. Lower-growing European annual species such as *L. hirsutus* and *L. pilosus* were also popular in the nineteenth-century garden

and seed is probably still obtainable. Seed. Up to
2m/6ft (perennials); up to 1.5m/5ft (annuals).
PAGE 64.

LYCHNIS Caryophyllaceae
HERBACEOUS BORDER **HP**

Campion, Catchfly Far less widely grown today in
gardens than their relatives, the pinks and carnations, these rather assertively red-flowered plants are
probably most familiar through the native British *L.
flos-cuculi*, Ragged Robin. But several other species
were popular in the nineteenth century, often in
double forms, including the two grown at Seggieden,
the red-flowered eastern Asian *L. chalcedonica*
(Maltese Cross) and the rare British native *L.
viscaria* (German Catchfly). Both are still available
as seed. 1m/3ft. PAGES 41, 100, 124.

LYSIMACHIA Primulaceae
HERBACEOUS BORDER **HP**

A large genus, generally under-used as garden plants
although there are many valuable species for moist
borders and bog gardens. Perhaps the most familiar
is Creeping Jenny, *L. nummularia*, a low-growing
British plant whose yellow flowers have long been
familiar at poolsides. Another yellow-flowered
native, *L. vulgaris*, the Yellow Loosestrife (about
30-90cm/1-3ft) is an undistinguished but useful
and easily grown plant for the middle of the border.
Rather more appealing is the species grown at Seggieden, the Japanese *L. clethroides* (1m/3ft), introduced in 1869 and bearing an almost buddleia-like
head of small white flowers. All three are available as
seed. PAGES 54, 101.

LYTHRUM Lythraceae
HERBACEOUS BORDER, BOG GARDEN **HP**

Loosestrife Quite unrelated to *Lysimachia* but in part
sharing a common name, the purple loosestrife is a
stately native species for moist conditions. The true
species is easily obtained as seed, but named cultivars
also exist. The commonest of these is 'Rosy Gem',
of uncertain age. Seed. 1.5m/5ft. PAGE 100.

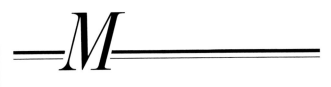

MAHONIA Berberidaceae
SHRUBBERY **S (s-l)**

A useful genus of evergreen Asian or North American
shrubs, closely related to *Berberis*. The commonest,
easiest, hardiest, most useful and almost longest
cultivated is the plant grown at Seggieden, *M. aquifolium*, the Oregon Grape. This is an invaluable
shrub of up to 2m/6ft for shady, dry, difficult conditions. Choose the species, not the rather more
floriferous modern 'Apollo'. Most of the other lovely
species and hybrids such as *M. lomariifolia* and
'Charity' are modern introductions but two closely
related and frequently confused eastern Asian
species, *M. bealii* and *M. japonica*, were both here
in the nineteenth century. Plants. PAGE 96.

MALVA Malvaceae
HERBACEOUS BORDER **HA/HP**

Mallow The Musk Mallow, *M. moschata*, a native
British plant of singularly undistinguished appearance, has long been cultivated for its rather loose pink
flowers, supported on disproportionately tall, leafy
stems. It typifies, however, the widespread use of
native plants in the Victorian period and earlier.
Seed. 70-90cm/2ft 4in-3ft. PAGE 80.

MECONOPSIS Papaveraceae
HERBACEOUS BORDER **HP**

The name *Meconopsis* today conjures up
M. betonicifolia, *M. grandis* and related
species of blue Himalayan Poppy. Apart from
some variants of *M. napaulensis* (1852), almost
all of these glorious forms date as garden plants
from the very end of the nineteenth or early
twentieth century. In Victorian gardens, the
native yellow-flowered Welsh Poppy
M. cambrica, was the species to be found.
Seed. 60cm/2ft.

**Meconopsis napaulensis
(Blue Himalayan poppy)**

131

III

IV

Pyrus Japonica
Japan Apple tree

I

II

V

Anemone
sulphurea
(Alpine Wind-
flower)

VI

Cardamine Trifolia
(Three leaved
cuckow Flower)

Anemone apennine
(Apennine Windflowe)

I *Cardamine trifolia*   **II** *Primula* sp. · Primrose   **III** *Narcissus* sp. · Daffodil
IV *Chaenomeles (= Pyrus) japonica* · Japan apple tree, Japanese quince
V *Pulsatilla alpina sulphurea (= Anemone sulphurea)* · Windflower
VI *Anemone apennina*

Narcissus sp. · Daffodils and narcissi

MERTENSIA Boraginaceae
ROCK GARDEN, SHADE GARDEN **HP**

Virginian Cowslip *Mertensia virginica* was and is the best species of this small group of predominantly blue-flowered low-growing herbs, similar and related to the more familiar pulmonarias. It is a useful plant for moist, shady corners. Seed. 50cm/20in. PAGE 25.

MIMULUS Scrophulariaceae
HERBACEOUS BORDER, BOG GARDEN **HP**

Musk A curious story attaches to *M. moschatus*, the Monkey Musk, a North American plant introduced to Britain in 1826 and now naturalized here. It was an indispensable species of the Victorian garden, its pale yellow flowers colouring the moist border and filling it with the aroma of musk. The plant is still grown but since 1914, unaccountably, it has been scentless, presumably because only certain forms were scented and for some reason these died out. The South American *M. luteus* was introduced at the same time but unfortunately does not have the same aroma. Both are still obtainable but modern seed catalogues abound with ghastly F_1 and other hybrids which should be avoided. Seed. 10-45cm/4-18in.

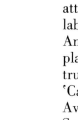

***Mimulus* sp. (Musk)**

MONARDA Labiatae
HERBACEOUS BORDER **HP**

Bergamot, Oswego Tea, Bee Balm One of the more attractive members of a huge group of aromatic labiates grown today in the herb garden, the North American *M. didyma* and related species are useful plants for the front of the border. Try to obtain the true species but, failing this, grow a form called 'Cambridge Scarlet', often offered by herb nurseries. Avoid the modern 'Panorama' and other mixtures. Seed or plants. 75-120cm/2ft 6in-4ft. PAGE 101.

MUSCARI Liliaceae
ROCK GARDEN, CONTAINERS, FRONT OF BORDER **HP**

Grape Hyacinth The commonest of the small, blue-flowered species grown today is *M. botryoides* from southern and eastern Europe, a plant that can rapidly become invasive. It was grown at Seggieden, alongside the more attractive, very dark-coloured but significantly less hardy *M. commutatum* from Sicily. But perhaps loveliest of all is the southern European Tassel Hyacinth, *M. comosum*, with much looser heads of intensely purple flowers. Bulbs. 10-25cm/6-10in. PAGES 17, 77, 152.

MYOSOTIS Boraginaceae
WOODLAND GARDEN, ROCK GARDEN **HA/HP**

Forget-Me-Not There are many species of these charming little blue-flowered plants, although some are lax and notoriously prone to mildew. Perhaps the commonest in Britain is the native *M. sylvatica*, seen at its best in semi-wild woodland areas, although the Mountain Forget-me-not, *M. alpestris*, is a more compact species. *M. scorpioides*, the Water Forget-me-not, is appropriate for the bog garden. Seed. 20cm/8in.

NARCISSUS Amaryllidaceae
HERBACEOUS BORDER, GRASS, CONTAINERS **HP**

Narcissi (including the long-trumpeted forms usually called daffodils) have been cultivated for centuries. During that time, tens of thousands of cultivars derived from many of the fifty or so wild species have been raised. The genus is now sub-divided into several groups or divisions (trumpet daffodils, double narcissi, poeticus narcissi and so forth) and most groups contain many cultivars. As with other very popular garden flowers, new narcissus cultivars have tended to oust most of the old ones and many of the modern classics such as the Copelands and the various pinks date from the early twentieth century. The following, however, are a few of the loveliest of the authentically Victorian daffodils that are still available, having proved their durability: 'Weardale Perfection', 'Empress', the two-toned 'W.P. Milner' and, most splendid of all, the rich golden 'King Alfred', although this did not actually appear until 1899. Among other narcissi, you should certainly have the old 'Pheasant's Eye'. Bulbs. 45cm/18in. PAGES 16, 20, 29, 109, 116, 132, 133.

OENOTHERA Onagraceae
HERBACEOUS BORDER **HB/HP**

Evening Primrose A very large genus of American herbaceous annuals, biennials, perennials and small shrubs with large, flamboyant flowers that open in the evening and are either loved or loathed. Many were introduced to British gardens throughout the nineteenth century but I shall select just three that are still readily available. *O. missouriensis* is a dwarf species that was grown at Seggieden. Its stems are prostrate and its clear yellow flowers huge – up to 12cm/5in across. *O. biennis* is a taller species (75cm-1.5m/ 2ft 6in-5ft) with smaller yellow flowers and a somewhat loose, devil-may-care habit, while *O. odorata* is more or less shrubby, up to about 1.5m/5ft, with yellow flowers that gradually become red-tinged. Seed. PAGE 61.

Oenothera missouriensis (Evening primrose)

OMPHALODES Boraginaceae
FRONT OF BORDER **HP**

Navel-wort, Blue-eyed Mary *Omphalodes* is very evidently related to forget-me-nots but is much more appealing, with electric blue flowers and a neater and mildew-free habit. The two species probably longest in cultivation are *O. verna* and *O. linifolia*, both from southern Europe, although the most beautiful is unquestionably the nineteenth-century introduction, *O. cappadocica,* a delight for a shady corner. Seed or plants. 20cm/8in. PAGE 89.

OURISIA Scrophulariaceae
ROCK GARDEN **HP**

Small, drooping, trumpet-like red flowers with protruding creamy anthers characterize *O. coccinea* from Chile. The secret of its cultivation eluded gardeners until well into the nineteenth century but a moist though well-drained soil, some shelter and ensurance that the rhizomes are not buried should prove successful. Seed or plants. 20cm/8in. PAGE 44.

P

PAEONIA Paeoniaceae
HERBACEOUS BORDER **HP**

Paeony Every gardener knows the paeony although few realize the scope of the genus which embraces thirty-three species from Europe, Asia and western North America. The familiar herbaceous garden paeonies are mostly derived from two species – the East Asian *P. lactiflora*, cultivated in the West since the late-eighteenth century but for more than a thousand years in China, and/or *P. officinalis*, a European species, grown in Britain since the sixteenth century. Another of the herbaceous species grown at Seggieden was *P. tenuifolia*, noted particularly for its finely dissected foliage. Hybridizing during this century has produced a large number of cultivars, but some of those popular in the nineteenth century survive – despite Hibberd's assertion that they were 'gaudy, scentless and short-lived'. Among old paeonies of *P. officinalis* parentage are 'Old Double Crimson' or 'Rubra Plena' and the pale pink 'Rosea Plena'; and among the most popular old lactiflora paeonies still listed are 'Reine Hortense' (1857), 'Festiva Maxima' (1851), 'Felix Crousse' (1881), 'Mons. Jules Elie' (1888) and 'Adolphe Rousseau' (1890). Plants. Up to 1m/3ft.

Even more glorious than the herbaceous paeonies are the various shrubby or tree paeonies. Unfortunately, all are fairly tender and also rather demanding, for they require a fairly mild climate yet not one where they are likely to commence growth before the danger of spring frost has passed. Surprisingly, nonetheless, moutan paeonies (cultivars of *P. suffruticosa*) were grown at Seggieden, as they had been for centuries in China. Modern cultivar introductions from Japan (immediately recognizable by their Japanese names) have supplanted the numerous old types, almost all of which seem to be unobtainable and possibly extinct. However, you may be fortunate enough still to find such named European forms as 'Comtesse de Tuder' and 'Louise Mouchelet' (both double pink) and 'Bijou de Chusan' (double white). Plants. Up to 2m/6ft. PAGE 137.

Omphalodes linifolia (Navelwort)

Galtonia
(hyacinthus)
candicans

I

II

Potentilla
atrosanguinea
(Cinquefoil)

III

Coronilla varia

I *Galtonia candicans*   **II** *Potentilla atrosanguinea* · Cinquefoil
III *Coronilla varia* · Crown vetch

I *Paeonia 'Moutan'* · Japanese tree paeony II *Paeonia tenuifolia* · Paeony

PAPAVER Papaveraceae
HERBACEOUS BORDER **HA/HP**

Poppies Just as the wild poppy, *P. rhoeas*, has been part of fields and farmland for centuries, so its relatives and descendants have long graced our gardens. At Seggieden, two eighteenth-century introductions were grown – *P. nudicaule* (the Iceland Poppy) from the sub-Arctic, with white or yellow petals, and *P. orientale* from western Asia, with huge scarlet petals. Both species have been hybridized with several others and poppy cultivars today are a confusing mixture. The popular Shirley poppies (now available as singles and doubles in a wide range of colours) were bred from a chance finding of aberrant plants of *P. rhoeas* by one Rev. W. Wilks in the late nineteenth century, as an attempt to resurrect some of the forms and colours described and illustrated in the eighteenth century. For the Victorian garden, perhaps the best choice would be true species of the wild *P. rhoeas*, which could be allowed to self-seed, *P. nudicaule*, *P. orientale*, and a selection, if you can find them, of the true Shirley poppies – single, in pure colours from scarlet to white (not mauve) and with no black either on stamens or petals. Seed. 30-90cm/1-3ft. PAGES 61, 145.

Pelargonium zonale

PELARGONIUM Geraniaceae
BEDDING **HHA**

Still confused with their predominantly hardy relatives, the geraniums, pelargoniums are plants of mainly South African origin that have become quite indispensable in summer bedding, windowboxes and containers. Several species have contributed to the recognized main types of regal, zonal and ivy-leaved. They first became extensively grown with the more widespread use of glasshouses in the early part of the nineteenth century, and the recent development of F_1 hybrids that can be raised from seed to flower in the first year has expanded their range beyond recognition. Although perennial, they are grown outdoors as half-hardy annuals, the stock plants (in the traditional manner) being over-wintered under protection, and cuttings taken either in early autumn or early spring. For the Victorian garden, the main problems relate to the choice of cultivars and to growing medium – the old types were selected for growing in soil-based mixtures and many do not thrive well in modern peat-based preparations. Today's F_1 hybrids are of course unacceptable, but the date of introduction of many old cultivars is not well recorded. However, the following zonals are all still obtainable, and were raised either late in the nineteenth century or very shortly afterwards: 'A.M. Mayne' (double, deep purple with scarlet flush), 'Gustav Emich' (semi-double, red-orange), 'Jewel' (double, deep rose-pink with white eye) and 'King of Denmark' (semi-double, salmon-pink). Plants. 30cm/12in.

PENSTEMON Scrophulariaceae
HERBACEOUS BORDER **HP**

Although the dwarf, hardy alpine species are useful plants for the rock garden, the American border penstemon, *P. barbatus* (sometimes called *Chelone barbata*) was particularly popular in the nineteenth-century garden, as at Seggieden. However, they require a sheltered place and are not reliably hardy in all northern situations. Mixed modern hybrids are readily available but so is the true species, a branched, 1m/3ft tall plant with pinkish flowers. Seed. PAGE 33.

PERILLA Labiatae
BEDDING **HHA**

One of the forgotten bedding plants, perilla is a highly aromatic labiate, the leaves of which are used to make a scented drink in the Far East. Forms of the shrubby *P. frutescens*, propagated by cuttings and cut back to give a carpet bronze-purple foliage in bedding displays, would add a real touch of authenticity to a Victorian planting. Unfortunately, seed is difficult to obtain in Britain. 30cm/12in (by cutting back).

PERNETTYA Ericaceae
SHRUBBERY **S (d-s)**

Several species of these attractive berrying dwarf shrubs for the peaty garden were introduced to Britain from South America, New Zealand and Tasmania in the nineteenth century. The commonest and easiest to grow is *P. mucronata*, an extremely hardy species brought back from Chile and neighbouring areas in 1828. Although notionally hermaphrodite, it is sensible to plant one named male form with every three females to ensure berry production. A suitable nineteenth-century female cultivar would be 'Alba', interplanted with the plant usually described simply as 'Male Form'. Plants. 75cm-1.5m/ 2ft 6in-5ft. PAGE 88.

PETASITES Compositae
HERBACEOUS BORDER **HP**

Winter Heliotrope *Petasites fragrans*, formerly grouped in *Tussilago*, is a dangerous plant to cultivate, for like its close relative, Butterbur, *P. hybridus*, it is rampant and invasive. Consequently it is seldom seen today, although it was an important contributor of perfume to the winter garden in Victorian times. The aroma is almost vanilla-like and the flowers reasonably attractive, small and white. Grow it, but confine it. Seed. 15cm/6in.

PETUNIA Solanaceae
BEDDING **HHA**

Yet another shrubby perennial grown in gardens as a half-hardy annual, the petunia has changed beyond recognition in its culture in recent years. The modern bedding petunias are the results of extensive breeding from the two South American species, the purple-flowered *P. integrifolia* and the white-flowered *P. nyctaginiflora*. However, in the Victorian garden, named varieties were propagated from cuttings taken in spring from overwintered stock plants. These

Petunia grandiflora

types have, of course, long gone and even in the nineteenth century the petunia was recognized as a problem plant in wet seasons. Given that some garish modern colour forms are fair mimics of the garish old types, then grow the 'Resisto' cultivars, which will stand up to wet weather fairly well. Seed. 15-25cm/6-10in.

PHILADELPHUS Hydrangeaceae
SHRUBBERY **S (s-l)**

Mock Orange Among the easiest grown, loveliest and most delightfully perfumed of all spring-flowering shrubs, philadelphuses have been recognized for many years as valuable plants for a sunny garden. Among the sixty-five species are several only introduced to gardens in this century. However, *P. coronarius*, the only European species and almost overpoweringly perfumed, has been grown in Britain for 300 years. The forms called 'Aureus' and 'Variegatus' are both very old. Only the very astute nineteenth-century gardener would have known the numerous hybrids, especially those of the Lemoine group, which were bred in France in the years following 1883; but they are so beautiful that the inclusion of the truly nineteenth-century types such as 'Lemoinei' (1888) and 'Manteau d'Hermine' (1898) must be justified. Sadly, the purist Victorian must exclude 'Virginal' (1909) and 'Belle Etoile' (1923). Plants. Up to 4m/13ft. PAGE 44.

PHLOMIS Labiatae
HERBACEOUS BORDER, SHRUBBERY **HP/S (s)**

Jerusalem Sage To many gardeners, including me, these are coarse and ugly plants, their form out of proportion to their size, but coarseness and ugliness were no strangers to the Victorians and the yellow-flowered Mediterranean *P. fruticosa* has been cultivated in sunny English gardens since the sixteenth century. Plants. 1-1.5m/3-5ft. PAGE 76.

PHLOX Polemoniaceae
HERBACEOUS BORDER, ROCK GARDEN **HP**

Among the loveliest and most reliable of all herbaceous perennials, the border phlox has the great merit of stout self-supporting stems that even today,

Petasites fragrans (**Winter heliotrope**)

thank goodness, plant hybridists have not managed to breed out. The modern plant is derived from the North American *P. paniculata* and occurs in a wide range of colours, although white, pink and the original deep purple are the most attractive. Apparently, the nineteenth-century cultivars have all gone, but a selection of modern forms would not be aggressively different. Plants. Up to 1.5m/5ft.

The dwarf rock garden or bedding phlox are wholly different in character from their larger brethren, but species such as *P. subulata* or its close relative *P. nivalis*, together with *P. drummondii* (although this can be very invasive) should certainly be included, preferably as true species for there are many modern cultivars and hybrids. Sadly, the Drummond-Hays do not seem to have grown *P. drummondii* at Seggieden. Seed or plants. Up to 45cm/18in. PAGES 41, 60, 93.

Phlox subulata (Moss pink)

PIERIS Ericaceae
SHRUBBERY S (s-l)

The commonest *Pieris* seen today is *P. formosa* and the form called 'Forest Flame', probably related to it. *P. formosa* was a late nineteenth-century introduction to Britain from the Himalayas, while 'Forest Flame' is a very recent natural hybrid with *P. japonica* as one parent. For the Victorian garden, a better choice in an acid, sheltered corner would be the small North American shrub, *P. floribunda*, once called *Andromeda floribunda*. The larger flowered selection known as 'Elongata' is twentieth-century. Plants. 1-2m/3-6ft. PAGE 17.

POLEMONIUM Polemoniaceae
HERBACEOUS BORDER **HP**

Jacob's Ladder *Polemonium coeruleum* is a native British plant that has been used in gardens for several centuries without ever causing great excitement. The flowers of the wild plant are blue but other colour selections now occur, although only the white seems very old. Seed. 1m/3ft. PAGE 28.

**Polygonatum multiflorum
(Solomon's seal)**

POLYGONATUM Polygonaceae
HERBACEOUS BORDER **HP**

Solomon's Seal *Polygonatum* is a large genus, allied to the even larger and generally weedier *Polygonum*, but one indispensable member is *P. multiflorum*, the common Solomon's Seal. It will tolerate the driest, shadiest conditions with impunity. Plants or seed. 1.5m/5ft.

PORTULACA Portulacaceae
BEDDING **HHA**

Purslane The decline in popularity of the South American *P. grandiflora* may have removed many of the old cultivars, but at least the plant has in consequence not been swamped by the F_1 hybrid brigade. It is a most undemanding little annual, although one that appreciates sun and a fairly poor soil. There are several named forms, most in shades of red and pink, although 'Thorburnii' is an old yellow. These types may no longer be available, so choose a modern mixture of singles. Seed. 15cm/6in.

POTENTILLA Rosaceae
HERBACEOUS BORDER **HP**

Mention potentillas to modern gardeners and they will think immediately of the small to medium sized shrubs such as 'Red Ace', 'Goldfinger' and 'Princess'; all cultivars of the native *P. fruticosa* and related species. These are all recent developments although the species is an old garden plant. In the Victorian garden, however, the herbaceous species were important too and typical among those readily available are the red flowered Himalayan *P. argyrophylla* and the closely related *P. atrosanguinea*. Seed. 90cm/3ft. PAGE 136.

PRIMULA Primulaceae
ROCK GARDEN, FRONT OF HERBACEOUS BORDER **HP**

The primroses, primulas, polyanthuses and auriculas make up a huge and important group of garden plants, including many hybrids of complex parentage, about which I have space only to generalize. The Wild Primrose *Primula vulgaris* must of course be grown, but it is in its double forms that the Victorian garden is best evoked. Considerable efforts have been made in recent years to find and resurrect some of these old cultivars, and specialist nurseries now offer several. Little need be said of the vulgar multicoloured modern polyanthus mixtures such as the 'Pacific' strain, but seek out the gorgeous laced forms like 'Gold Lace' and such other old types (for instance, those of 'Jack in the Green' and 'Hose in Hose' form) as you can find. The exquisite cultivars derived from the European alpine *P. auricula* became immensely important during the nineteenth century, and a virtual cult developed in growing the 'Show' auriculas in pots under cover, their flowers protected from the rain. Auriculas, too, have seen a modest revival in recent years, and a small selection of the rather more robustly flowered old border cultivars may fairly easily be obtained. Seeds or plants. Up to 60cm/2ft. PAGES 15, 17, 52, 80, 88, 93, 96, 116, 132, 152.

PRUNUS Rosaceae
SHRUBBERY, SPECIMEN **T(s)**

The genus *Prunus* is most frequently represented in modern gardens by plum trees, of course, and by a range of generally assertive and vulgar Japanese cherries, of which 'Kanzan' is unaccountably the most popular. Because most of these cherries were not introduced to Britain until the early years of the present century, the Victorians boasted a more tasteful array. Perhaps the best choice for the nineteenth-century garden would be a selection from *P. dulcis* 'Roseoplena' (Double Almond), cultivated in the basic form since the sixteenth century; *P. davidiana* (David's Peach: 1865), in a sheltered spot; *P. laurocerasus* (Cherry Laurel: seventeenth century) – not attractive but very characteristic; *P. mahaleb* (Saint Lucie Cherry: 1714); and *P. spinosa* (the native Wild Sloe or Blackthorn). Plants. Up to 8m/25ft. PAGES 20, 28, 85, 109.

PULMONARIA Boraginaceae
HERBACEOUS BORDER, WOODLAND GARDEN **HP**

Lungwort These blue-flowered perennials are under-valued today when more subtle things are available, but the pulmonarias are very hardy, somewhat coarse but extremely useful plants for shady corners, where they will spread agreeably yet not uncontrollably. *P. longifolia* and *P. officinalis* are both British natives and acceptable enough, although the selected forms of the introduced *P. angustifolia*, including the white 'Alba', are better; the excellent 'Munstead' is presumably a Jekyll plant, although of uncertain date. Plants. 30cm/12in. PAGE 108.

Pulmonaria saccharata (Lungwort)

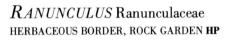

RANUNCULUS Ranunculaceae
HERBACEOUS BORDER, ROCK GARDEN **HP**

A garish range of cultivar mixtures derived from *R. asiaticus* is to be found in modern seed catalogues; and in the nineteenth century, numerous named and equally garish forms were likewise popular. But the name *Ranunculus* means more to the alpine enthusiast who grows such species as *R. amplexicaulis* and is challenged by others such as *R. glacialis*. Many of the alpine forms have been cultivated for many years and were certainly at home in the Victorian rock garden. Yet other species and types were also popular – for instance, Bachelor's Buttons, a double form of *R. acris*, the Meadow Buttercup, as well as white and other variants of *R. ficaria*, the Lesser Celandine. Some of these are still available but should be placed with caution as they can become invasive. Seed. Up to 30cm/12in. PAGE 20.

RHODODENDRONS Ericaceae
SHRUBBERY **S (s-l)**

The rhododendrons need no introduction, and it was during the late nineteenth and early twentieth century that the parents of so many of our familiar modern hybrids were sent home from Asia. Nonetheless, hybridizing had begun as long ago as 1825, using *R. arboreum* as one parent. Given a shaded, peaty soil, and a fairly large garden (the dwarfer rhododendrons were scarcely available before this century), a suitable small selection of the more manageable types

Primula vulgaris (Common primrose)

Primula vulgaris 'Flore Pleno' (Double-flowered primrose)

for the Victorian garden would be *R. campanulatum* (3m/10ft: 1825); *R. campylocarpum* (3m/10ft: 1849); *R. catawbiense* (3m/10ft: 1809); *R. dauricum* (2m/6ft: 1780 – grown at Seggieden); *R. hirsutum* (1m/3ft: 1656 – the longest cultivated rhododendron); *R. ponticum* (7m/23ft: 1763 – now naturalized to weed status in some areas); and, for hybrids, 'Ascot Brilliant' (about 2m/6ft: 1862, crimson with black flecks); 'Cynthia' (up to 7m/23ft: 1862, deep rose-pink with darker spots); 'Jacksonii' (2m/6ft: 1835, rose pink with darker and paler flecks); 'Lady Eleanor Cathcart' (7m/23ft: about 1836, clear pink with maroon markings); and 'Madame Masson' (3m/10ft: 1849, white with yellow blotches). Plants. PAGES 28, 40, 88, 89.

RIBES Grossulariaceae
SHRUBBERY S (s-m)

Currant The flowering currants are forms of the North American *R. sanguineum* which was introduced to Britain in 1826 and soon became very popular. They are not everyone's choice, tending to be gaunt if the old wood is not pruned out regularly; nevertheless, they bring a welcome splash of spring colour, but modern cultivars such as 'Pulborough Scarlet' should be avoided. The white 'Albidum' originated in Scotland around 1840 and was especially appropriate at Seggieden, but among other old cultivars are the crimson 'Atrorubens', the double red 'Flore Pleno' and the pink and white 'Carneum Grandiflorum'. Plants. 3m/10ft. PAGES 53, 108.

RUDBECKIA Compositae
HERBACEOUS BORDER HP

Cone Flower, Black-eyed Susan Several species of North American *Rudbeckia* have found their way into British gardens; *R. laciniata* (2m/6ft), the perennial Cone Flower, is one of the oldest in cultivation, having been grown in England since about 1640, with the annual *R. hirta* (75cm/2ft 6in), Black-eyed Susan, following in 1714. Modern dwarf hybrids dominate catalogues today but the true species are still sometimes obtainable. Seed.

Rudbeckia laciniata
(Cone flower)

S

SANGUINARIA Papaveraceae
HERBACEOUS BORDER HP

Bloodroot One of the neglected plants of the past, the North American *S. canadensis* was popular in British gardens from the seventeenth to the nineteenth century. It is appreciated for its low-growing, creeping habit and delightful white spring flowers, but its position must be well marked for it soon disappears from view after blooming. Easily the most attractive form is the double 'Flore Pleno', of uncertain age. Plants or seed. 15cm/6in. PAGE 77.

SAPONARIA Caryophyllaceae
ROCK GARDEN, FRONT OF BORDER HP

Soapwort Among the various species of *Saponaria*, only one is worth serious consideration: *S. ocymoides*, a European alpine with attractive small pink flowers that will tumble happily over walls and rocks. It makes a pleasant and welcome change from *Aubrieta*. The often recommended border species, *S. officinalis*, is too invasive to trust. Seed. 15cm/6in.

Saponaria ocymoides

SAXIFRAGA Saxifragaceae
ROCK GARDEN HP

Saxifrage Indispensable for any rock or wall garden, saxifrages are now available in a bewildering range of species and cultivars. The Victorians knew the worth of these lovely alpines but had a very much poorer cultivar selection from which to choose. The expert alpine gardener will wish to delve deeper into the history of the cultivation of this genus, but a token collection could include the two species grown at Seggieden, *S. oppositifolia* and *S. wallacei* (= *camposii*). Plants. 15cm/6in. PAGES 21, 52.

SCABIOSA Dipsacaceae
HERBACEOUS BORDER **HP**

Scabious William Robinson called *S. caucasica* 'the finest perennial in my garden'. Certainly, its dense blue flower heads are appealing, although most nineteenth-century gardeners would also have selected the annual *S. atropurpurea*, the Sweet Scabious, which obviously found popularity at Seggieden. Normally with deep purple flowers, white and yellowish single and double forms exist. Mixed hybrids of both are obtainable today. Seed. 45-60cm/18-24in. PAGE 61.

SCHIZOSTYLIS Iridaceae
HERBACEOUS BORDER **HP**

Kaffir Lily The South African *S. coccinea* has had its devotees since it was first introduced to Britain in 1864. The spike of rather spreading scarlet flowers with yellow anthers makes a welcome addition to the border in autumn, but a warm, sheltered corner is needed. There are also pink-flowered cultivars, of uncertain age. Rhizomes. 1m/3ft. PAGE 120.

SCILLA Liliaceae
FRONT OF BORDER, ROCK GARDEN **HP**

Squill There is no better welcome to the spring than that offered by the bright blue of scillas. *S. siberica* is the lovelier and slightly smaller of the two common species, *S. bifolia* being the other. However, the genus is a very large one, with around ninety species, and many other European and Asian types were cultivated both outdoors and in greenhouses during the nineteenth century. There are old white forms of both *S. bifolia* and *S. siberica* and an old pink form of the former. bulbs. 15cm/6in. PAGES 88, 97, 109.

SCOPOLIA Solanaceae
HERBACEOUS BORDER **HP**

You will need to search both gardeners' memories and nurseries to find scopolias today, but these rather low-growing eastern European perennials with nodding green or purplish flowers were once common in British gardens. *S. carniolica* is the species to look for. Seed. 35cm/14in. PAGE 77.

SEDUM Crassulaceae
ROCK GARDEN **HP**

Stonecrop Like *Saxifraga*, *Sedum* is a large and complicated genus of rock garden plants, some of which are recent, others ancient, some neat and compact and others sprawling and invasive. A token collection of species cultivated during the nineteenth century could include *S. reflexum*, *S. acre*, *S. villosum* and *S. anglicum*. Seed or plants. 15cm/6in. PAGE 104.

Sempervivum arachnoides (Houseleek)

SEMPERVIVUM Crassulaceae
ROCK GARDEN, BEDDING **HP**

Houseleeks Much of my comment about sedums is applicable to the related sempervivums, although the genus is rather smaller and this is a group of plants that was also very important in bedding displays. The neat, compact rosettes of such species as the naturalized *S. tectorum* were found especially valuable in providing a neat edging. Buy seed of mixtures and select those forms most attractive and appealing for bedding purposes. Seed or plants. 10cm/4in.

SILENE Caryophyllaceae
HERBACEOUS BORDER, ROCK GARDEN **HP**

Campion, Catchfly *Silene* is very closely related and similar to *Lychnis*, and in Victorian gardening books some species will be found to flit from one genus to the other. Among those placed in *Silene* today and widely grown then are the neat, moss-like alpine species such as *S. acaulis*, the Moss Campion, and the taller-growing, hairy, white-flowered border perennial, *S. fimbriata* (1m/3ft). Seed or plants.

Schizostylis coccinea (Kaffir lily)

Thalictrum flavum
(Meadow rue)

SISYRINCHIUM Iridaceae
FRONT OF BORDER, ROCK GARDEN **HP**

Although a very large genus, few species of these graceful plants have become popular in gardens. The main exception is *S. douglasii*, often called *S. grandiflorum*, an elegant grass-like plant with purple, pink or white bell-like flowers in early summer. Seed. 30cm/12in. PAGE 108.

SOLIDAGO Compositae
HERBACEOUS BORDER **HP**

Golden Rod Unfortunately, the tall, weedy North American *S. canadensis* was such a common inhabitant of the nineteenth-century garden that it cannot be ignored. Dwarf forms such as 'Baby Gold' are modern hybrids derived from related species. Seed. 2m/6ft. PAGE 33.

SYMPHORICARPOS Caprifoliaceae
SHRUBBERY **S (s-m)**

Snowberry The North American *S. albus*, especially in its variety *laevigatus* (sometimes called *S. rivularis*), has been a popular if undramatic garden shrub since the early nineteenth century. The real merit lies in the snow-white berries that ripen in the autumn and are usually left alone by birds. Plants. 2m/6ft. PAGE 72.

TANACETUM Compositae
HERBACEOUS BORDER **HP**

Pyrethrum The genus *Tanacetum* is now the resting place for the plant long known as *Pyrethrum*; another species, the Feverfew, departs periodically to *Chrysanthemum*. Pyrethrums are useful aromatic border perennials. The insecticide pyrethrum is obtained from *T. cinerariifolium*. The more common garden plant, popular in the nineteenth century, is *T. coccineum*, a red, white and yellow flowered daisy-like perennial. The many named cultivars seem to be no more, and a modern mixture (listed as pyrethrum in catalogues) must suffice. Seed. 60cm/2ft. PAGE 45.

THALICTRUM Ranunculaceae
HERBACEOUS BORDER **HP**

Meadow Rue Although a large genus, few species have become significant garden plants until recent times when cultivars of the Chinese *T. dipterocarpum* have attained some popularity. This was unknown in the nineteenth century, but a home in the herbaceous border was found for the native *T. flavum* (1m/3ft) and the prettier, more delicately foliaged and extraordinarily variable *T. minus* (1m/3ft), a useful plant as ground cover under shrubs. Seed.

TIARELLA Saxifragaceae
FRONT OF BORDER, ROCK GARDEN, WOODLAND **HP**

Foam Flower *Tiarella cordifolia* from North America was introduced to Britain in the early eighteenth century and its masses of star-like white flowers and spreading habit soon became appreciated. However, care is needed to keep it within bounds. A form 'Purpurea' with reddish flowers seems to be old. *T. wherryi*, often offered today, is recent. Seed. 30cm/12in. PAGE 40.

TRADESCANTIA Commelinaceae
FRONT OF BORDER **HP**

Spider-wort Although tradescantias are perhaps better known today as house plants, the hardy North American *T. virginica* (or, more probably, a cross between this and *T. ohiensis*) has given rise to many useful low-growing garden cultivars. Hibberd wrote of about a dozen types but it is difficult to determine which of these survive. Certainly, the white 'Osprey', the blue and white 'Iris Pritchard' and the blue 'Leonora' are fairly old. Plants. 45cm/18in. PAGE 44.

TRILLIUM Liliaceae
WOODLAND **HP**

Wood Lily There are few more lovely plants for the woodland garden or shaded border than these strange, broad-leaved members of the lily family. Two fine North American species grew at Seggieden, the white or faintly pinkish-flowered *T. grandiflorum* (45cm/18in) and the dark purple *T. erectum*. Seed or plants. PAGES 20, 29.

I *Weigela grandiflora*   II *Jasminum pubigerum*
III *Papaver orientale* · Oriental poppy

TRITELEIA Liliaceae
HERBACEOUS BORDER **HP**

Some of the grassy-leaved species of *Brodiaea*, including the plant now usually called *Ipheion uniflora*, which grew at Seggieden, have often been grouped in the related genus *Triteleia*. The present species (a bulb, not a corm) has delicate, rather star-like flowers ranging from white to purple, and most of the variants seem to have been cultivated for a long time; however, the very dark and lovely form called 'Froyle Mill' is recent. Bulbs. 30cm/12in. PAGES 97, 117.

TROLLIUS Ranunculaceae
HERBACEOUS BORDER, BOG GARDEN **HP**

Globe Flower One of the loveliest of native British flowers, *T. europaeus* has been cultivated for centuries and during much of this time has existed in several forms, including the one grown at Seggieden. This is called *napellifolius*, a strong-growing plant with many-flowered stems and very deeply dissected leaves. Hybrids are often offered today, but these are the results of crosses between the native plant and *T. chinensis*, a twentieth-century introduction. Seed or plants. 50cm/20in. PAGE 21.

TROPAEOLUM Tropaeolaceae
BEDDING, ON SUPPORTS **HHA**

Flame Flower There are essentially two main types of tropaeolums (or nasturtiums, as they are still sometimes called) and two principal uses for them. From *T. minus*, introduced from Peru as long ago as 1585,

Tropaeolum peltophorum

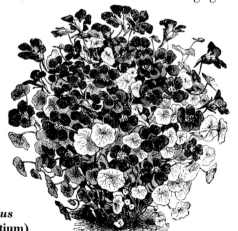

***Tropaeolum majus*
'Tom Thumb' (Nasturtium)**

come the fairly compact bedding types of which the 'Tom Thumb' strain (30cm/12in) is the best known. It is still freely available but may differ from the 'Tom Thumb' plants known to the Victorians. Better known and more useful are the climbing types, derived from *T. majus*, *T. peltophorum* and *T. peregrinum* (Canary Creeper) and which attain 6m/20ft or more. Today the best plan is probably to opt for 'Tall Mixed (Climbing)' – and remember that the sunnier the site and the poorer the soil, the better will they thrive. Seed.

TULIPA Liliaceae
BEDDING, HERBACEOUS BORDER **HP**

Tulips The fluctuations in the tulip's popularity and the 'tulipomania' craze of the early eighteenth century have been well documented. In recent years, the numbers of cultivars, mostly from Holland and, latterly, the numbers of species on offer have become quite bewildering. From this multiplicity of bloom, I can merely suggest simple guidelines for growing tulips in a nineteenth-century setting. You will do far worse than concentrate on the May-flowering Breeder tulips, with cup-shaped flowers in which the base of the flower is white or yellow in the English forms but often stained with a darker colour as well in the Dutch types. Although other tulips were grown in gardens, these can be said to be the most characteristic tulip flower types of the period. The choice of cultivars must be dictated by those that are obtainable; a reputable bulb supplier should be able to suggest a selection of old types from his list but failing these, modern May-flowering tulips of the type described would suffice. Bulbs. PAGE 148.

V·W

VERBENA Verbenaceae
BEDDING **HHA**

Quite indispensable as a nineteenth-century bedding plant, yet never easy, would summarize the old verbenas. The plant generally called the Garden Verbena, *V.* × *hybrida*, is a complex hybrid involving several South American species and originated in the same year as another complex hybrid, Queen

Victoria, came to the throne. A wide range of variously coloured compact hybrids was raised subsequently and propagated by cuttings from over-wintered plants. But many stock plants were invariably lost each winter, and in hot, dry seasons, and in light soils, the bedding plants suffered badly. The advent, during the nineteenth century, of forms raised easily from seed was greatly welcomed. Probably the only truly old cultivar still available is the large and very vivid scarlet 'Firefly'. This aside, a modern mixture must suffice. Seed. 25cm/10in.

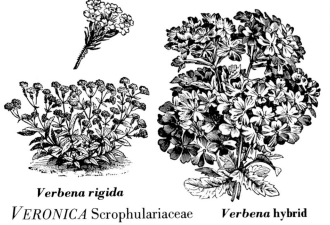

Verbena rigida

VERONICA Scrophulariaceae
HERBACEOUS BORDER **HP**

***Verbena* hybrid**

Speedwell This is a large genus of very varied form, ranging from many small, creeping and problematic weeds to the large, shrubby hebes. There are places for many of them in gardens, although they cannot always be trusted. Three herbaceous species would be appropriate: *V. incana*, *V. spicata* (both 45cm/18in), and the lower-growing *V. gentianoides*. There are modern cultivars of these but the true species are also available. Seed or plants. PAGES 81, 100, 108, 112, 113.

VIBURNUM Caprifoliaceae
SHRUBBERY **S (m-l)**

Viburnums are among the most valuable shrubs in a garden of any age but from the 150 evergreen and deciduous species, one above all must be included. The Mediterranean evergreen, *V. tinus* (3m/10ft), which was for long called laurustinus, is invaluable for its pink buds and white flowers that appear throughout the winter. Forced to select one more, it would be the wide-branching, spring-flowering deciduous Chinese shrub, *V. plicatum tomentosum* (3m/10ft), introduced by Robert Fortune around

1865. There are many selected forms such as 'Mariesii'; but all are post-Victorian and the original plant may require some searching for. Plants. PAGE 88.

VINCA Apocynaceae
SHRUBBERY, WOODLAND **S(d)**

Periwinkle There are few better ground cover plants, especially for dry shady areas, than the blue-flowered periwinkles of which the two best species occur wild (probably naturalized) in Britain. The most vigorous is *V. major* (45cm/18in) but the prettier is *V. minor* (15cm/6in). There are colour and leaf variants of both but all these appear to be twentieth-century introductions. Plants. PAGES 96, 116.

VIOLA Violaceae
BEDDING, CONTAINERS, WOODLAND **HA/HP**

Pansies, Violets, Violas There can be few more charming or friendly garden plants than violas, many having amusing and expressive face patterns on their petals. I can barely do justice to them but commend first the delightfully perfumed sweet violets, raised from several Asian species and giving rise in the nineteenth century to such cultivars as 'Czar', 'Duchess de Parme' and 'Perle Rose'. Specialist nurseries still supply these plants, together with the Parma violets, of less certain parentage and difficult cultivation. Among pansies, the Wild Heartsease *V. tricolor* is a must, together with a selection of the early pansy hybrids bred from this species and also from *V. cornuta*, *V. lutea* and *V. amoena*. Specialist nurseries will again be able to advise on the availability of old plants. Seed or plants. 15cm/6in. PAGES 16, 17, 29, 53, 97.

WEIGELA Caprifoliaceae
SHRUBBERY **S (s-m)**

Weigelas have probably never been more popular, largely as the result of the introduction of many new cultivars in recent years. The principal cultivated species were nonetheless introduced to Britain from China and Japan during the nineteenth century – *W. coraeensis* also called *grandiflora* (4m/13ft) and *W. middendorffiana* (2m/6ft) in 1850, and *W. florida* (3m/10ft) by Fortune in 1844. For authenticity, choose the true species only. Plants. PAGE 145.

***Viola* sp. (French pansies)**

***Viola tricolor* (Heartsease)**

Tulipa sp. · Tulips

I *Phygelius capensis* · Cape figwort   **II** *Digitalis grandiflora*
III *Gypsophila paniculata*

SUPPLIERS AND USEFUL ADDRESSES

The following list of nurseries and organizations should prove useful for locating suppliers of plants and seeds for the Victorian flower garden.

BRITISH ISLES

Abbeybrook Cactus Nursery,
Old Hackney Lane,
Matlock,
Derbyshire
Succulents

Allwood Bros.,
Clayton Nursery,
Hassocks,
West Sussex BN6 9LX
Carnations and pinks

David Austin Roses,
Bowling Green Lane,
Albrighton,
Wolverhampton WV7 3HB
Roses

Ayletts Nurseries,
North Orbital Road,
London Colney,
St Albans AL2 1DH
Dahlias

Helen Ballard,
Old Country,
Mathon,
Malvern,
Hereford and Worcester
Snowdrops and hellebores

Barnhaven,
Brigsteer,
Kendal,
Cumbria LA8 8AU
Primroses

Peter Beales Roses,
London Road,
Attleborough,
Norfolk NR17 1AY
Roses

Blackmore & Langdon,
Stanton Nurseries,
Pensford, Bristol BS18 4JL
Delphiniums and other herbaceous plants

Ann and Roger Bowden,
Sticklepath,
Okehampton,
Devon
Hostas

Broadleigh Gardens,
Barr House,
Bishops Hull,
Taunton,
Somerset TA4 1AE
Small bulbs

Carncairn Daffodil Ltd,
Carncairn Lodge,
Broughshane,
Ballymena,
Antrim,
N. Ireland BT43 7HF
Daffodils

Richard G. M. Cawthorne,
28 Trigon Road,
London SW8 1NK
Violas and violets

John Chambers,
15 Westleigh Road,
Barton Seagrave,
Kettering,
Northamptonshire NN15 5AJ
Wild flower seeds

The Beth Chatto Gardens,
White Barn House,
Elmstead Market,
Colchester,
Essex CO7 7DB
Unusual herbaceous plants

Chiltern Seeds,
Bortree Stile,
Ulverston,
Cumbria A12 7PB
Large selection of unusual, old or rare species

Jack Drake,
Inshriach Alpine Plant Nursery,
Aviemore,
Inverness
Alpine plants

Margery Fish Nursery,
East Lambrook Manor,
South Petherton,
Somerset TA13 5HL
Unusual herbaceous plants

Fisk's Clematis Nursery,
Westleton,
Saxmundham,
Suffolk IP17 3AJ
Clematis

Mr Fothergill's Seeds,
Gazeley Road,
Kentford,
Newmarket,
Suffolk CB8 7QB
General seeds

Glenhirst Nursery,
Station Road,
Swineshead, Boston,
Lincolnshire PE20 3NX
Succulents

Great Dixter Nurseries,
Northiam,
Sussex
Clematis, unusual herbaceous plants and shrubs

C.W. Groves & Son,
The Nurseries,
West Bay Road,
Bridport,
Dorset DT6 4BA
Old violets

Growing Carpets,
The Old Farmhouse,
Steeple Morden,
Royston,
Hertfordshire
Ground cover plants

Hartside Nursery Garden,
Alston,
Cumbria CA9 3BL
Alpines

Hayward's Carnations,
The Chace Gardens,
Stakes Road,
Purbrook,
Portsmouth PO7 5PL
Carnations and pinks

Hill's Fuchsias,
Hunwick Nurseries,
Hunwick Station,
Crook,
Co. Durham DL15 0RB
Fuchsias

Hillier Nurseries Ltd,
Ampfield House,
Ampfield,
Romsey,
Hampshire SO5 9PA
Trees and shrubs – probably most comprehensive in the world

Brenda Hyatt Auriculas,
1 Toddington Crescent,
Bluebell Hill,
Chatham,
Kent
Primulas and auriculas

W. E. Th. Ingwerson Ltd,
Birch Farm Nursery,
Gravetye,
East Grinstead,
West Sussex RH19 4LE
Alpines

Michael Jefferson-Brown,
Maylite,
Martley,
Hereford and Worcester
Daffodils

Kelways Nurseries,
Langport,
Somerset TA10 9SL
Herbaceous plants

Langthorns Plantery,
Little Canfield,
Dunmow,
Essex
*Unusual herbaceous plants
and shrubs*

C. S. Lockyer,
'Lansbury',
70 Henfield Road,
Coalpit Heath,
Bristol BS17 2UZ
Fuchsias

Old Court Nurseries,
Colwall,
Malvern,
Worcestershire WR13 6QE
Michaelmas daisies

Orchard Nurseries,
Foston,
Grantham,
Lincolnshire
Unusual herbaceous plants

Oscrofts,
Spotborough Road,
Doncaster,
Yorkshire DN5 8BE
Dahlias

J. & E. Parker-Jervis,
Marten's Hall Farm,
Longworth,
Abingdon,
Oxfordshire OX13 5EP
*Unusual hardy plants and
bulbs*

Pennyacre Nurseries,
Crawley House,
Springfield,
Fife KY15 5RU
Heathers

Polden Acres Gardens,
Broadway,
Edington,
Bridgwater,
Somerset TA7 9HA
Heathers

Rathowen Daffodils,
Knowehead,
Dergmoney,
Omagh,
Co. Tyrone,
N. Ireland
Daffodils

Rileys,
Alfreton Nurseries,
Woolley Moor,
Derbyshire DE5 6FF
Chrysanthemums

Roses du Temps Passe,
Woodlands House,
Stretton,
Stafford ST19 9LG
Roses

Elizabeth Smith,
Downside,
Bowling Green,
Constantine,
Falmouth,
Cornwall TR11 5AP
Violets

Suttons Seeds,
Hele Road,
Torquay,
Devon TQ2 7QJ
General seeds

Thompson & Morgan Ltd,
London Road,
Ipswich,
Suffolk TP2 0BA
General and unusual seeds

Thorp's Geraniums,
257 Finchampstead Road,
Wokingham,
Berkshire RG11 3JT
Pelargoniums

Treasures of Tenbury,
Burford House,
Tenbury Wells,
Hereford and Worcester
WR15 8HQ
*Clematis and unusual
shrubs and herbaceous
plants*

Van Tubergen,
304a Upper Richmond
Road West,
London SW14 7JG
Bulbs

USA

Appalachian Gardens,
PO Box 82,
Waynesboro,
PA 17268

Country Gardens,
74 South Road,
Pepperell,
MA 01463

Crownsville Nursery,
1241 Generalsway Hwy,
Crownsville,
MD 21032

Duo Herbs,
2015 Potshop Road,
Norristown,
PA 19403

Golden Meadow Herb Farm,
431 South St Augustine,
Dallas,
TX 75217

**McClure and Zimmerman
Bulbs,**
1422 W. Thorndale,
Chicago,
IL 60660

Meadowbrook Farm Nursery,
1633 Washington Lane,
Meadowbrook,
PA 19046

Merry Gardens,
Camden,
ME 04843

Midwest Wildflowers,
PO Box 644,
Rockton,
IL 61072

Moreau Landscape Nursery,
89 County Road East,
Colts Neck,
NJ 07722

Topiary Art Works,
PO Box 574,
Clearwater,
KS 67026

J. Th. de Vroomen Bulbs Co,
PO Box A 66140,
Chicago,
IL 60666

Waterloo Gardens,
136 Lancaster Avenue,
Devon,
PA 19333

White Flower Farm,
Litchfield,
CT 06759

AUSTRALIA

**Association of Societies for
Growing Australian Plants,**
c/o Post Office,
Shenton Park,
Western Australia 6008

**Canberra Horticultural Society
Inc,**
GPO Box 1388,
Canberra,
ACT 2601

**Horticultural Association of
South Australia,**
Box 43,
PO Rundle Mail,
South Australia 5000

**Queensland Council of Garden
Clubs,**
8 Martock Street,
Camp Hill,
Queensland 4152

**Royal Horticultural Society of
NSW,**
55 Railway Parade,
Peakhurst,
New South Wales 2601

**Royal Horticultural Society of
Victoria,**
418A Station Street,
Box Hill South,
Victoria 3128

**Western Australian
Horticultural Council,**
PO Box 135,
Claremont,
Western Australia 6010

CANADA

**Canadian Horticultural
Council,**
3 Amberwood Crescent,
Nepean ON K2E 7L1

**Canadian Society for
Horticultural Science,**
Agriculture Canada,
Research Station,
Box 1000,
Agassiz BC V0M 1A0

**Canadian Botanical
Association,**
Dept. of Botany,
University of Alberta,
Edmonton AB T6G 2E9

NEW ZEALAND

**Royal NZ Institute of
Horticulture Inc,**
PO Box 12,
Lincoln College,
Canterbury

SOUTH AFRICA

**The Botanical Society of
South Africa,**
Head Office,
Kirstenbosch,
Private Bag X7,
7735 Claremont,
Cape Province

**Orange Free State Botanic
Garden,**
PO Box 1536,
9300 Bloemfontein,
Orange Free State

Botanic Gardens,
Botanic Gardens Road,
4001 Durban,
Natal

**The Pretoria National
Botanic Garden,**
2 Cussonia Road,
Private Bag X101,
Brummeria,
0001 Pretoria,
(0184 for street address)
Transvaal

Muscari botryoides
(Grape Hyacinth)

I

II

III

IV

Primula acaulis
(Double primrose)

I *Crocus* (garden hybrids) · Large Dutch crocus
II *Muscari botryoides* · Grape hyacinth **III** *Erica herbacea* · Winter heather
IV *Primula* sp. · Double primrose

BIBLIOGRAPHY

The literature of the history of gardening is vast and the general literature of the Victorian age even more vast. The selected reading list that follows includes the most important and popular Victorian books on flower gardening and also those modern books most useful to anyone seeking to re-create a Victorian style of garden. Perhaps most valuable and fascinating of all, however, are the volumes of nineteenth-century gardening magazines and periodicals of which at least some should be available at any good reference library. Among the most useful of the British magazines and periodicals are 'Amateur Gardening', 'The Gardener's Chronicle and Agricultural Gazette', 'The Cottage Gardener and Country Gentleman's Companion', 'Gardening Illustrated' and 'The Gardener'.

Modern periodicals carry articles and advertisements relevant to re-creating a Victorian style of garden and locating the necessary plants from time to time, and in Britain 'The Garden' and 'The Plantsman' are among those to be recommended. More general, popular matter on the reconstruction and restoration of nineteenth-century buildings and gardens appears in 'Traditional Homes', while the specialist technical horticultural and architectural literature will attract the very keen enthusiast.

Societies exist to foster interest in particular groups of plants and many of these have groups concerned with their history. In Britain, information on specialist societies may be obtained through the Royal Horticultural Society. Existing under the RHS aegis is the important National Council for the Preservation of Plants and Gardens which seeks to conserve important gardens and plant varieties of all ages. In other countries, help may be obtained through state or national horticultural societies. American readers will find 'The Gardener's Book of Sources' by W.B. Logan (Penguin, 1988) useful for information on books, periodicals, nurseries and societies.

BOOKS

Beales, P., *Classic Roses*, 1985

Bean, W.J., *Trees and Shrubs Hardy in the British Isles*, 4 vols., Rev. Edn. 1970-80

Brickell, C. & Sharman, F., *The Vanishing Garden*, 1986

Carter, T., *The Victorian Garden*, 1984

Cobbett, W., *The English Gardener*, 1833

Delamer, E.S., *The Flower Garden*, 1860

Doyle, M., *The Flower Garden*, 1845

Ellacombe, H.N., *In a Gloucestershire Garden*, 1985

Fish, M., *Cottage Garden Flowers*, 1961

Genders, R., *Collecting Antique Plants*, 1971

Glenny, G., *The Culture of Flowers and Plants*, 1861

Glenny, G., *Handbook to the Flower Garden and Greenhouse*, 1851

Hadfield, M., *A History of British Gardening*, Rev. Edn. 1970

Hibberd, S., *The Amateur's Flower Garden*, 1871

Hibberd, S., *Familiar Garden Flowers*, 1898

Hiller's Manual of Trees and Shrubs, Rev. Edn. 1981

Hole, S.R., *A Book about Roses*, 1869

Hole, S.R., *A Book about the Garden*, 1892

Huxley, A., *An Illustrated History of Gardening*, 1978

Jekyll, G., *Colour Schemes for the Flower Garden*, 1908

Jekyll, G., *A Gardener's Testament*, 1937

Jekyll, G., *Wood and Garden*, 1899

Jekyll, G., *Home and Garden*, 1900

Loudon, J., *The Ladies' Companion to the Flower Garden*, 1846

Loudon, J.C., *The Cottager's Manual*, 1840

McIntosh, C., *The Flower Garden*, 1838

Robinson, W., *The Wild Garden*, 1870

Robinson, W., *Alpine Flowers for English Gardens*, 1870

Robinson, W., *The English Flower Garden*, 1883

Royal Horticultural Society, *Dictionary of Gardening*, 2nd. Edn. 1956

Scourse, N., *The Victorians and their Flowers*, 1983

Stuart, D. & Sutherland, J., *Plants from the Past*, 1987

Taylor, G., *The Victorian Flower Garden*, 1952

Thomas, G.S., *Recreating the Period Garden*, 1984

Thomson, D., *Handy Book of the Flower Garden*, 1868

Watts, E., *Flowers and the Flower Garden*, 1869

PLANT INDEX

GENERAL INDEX

Page numbers in *italic* refer to
illustrations